50 Cooperative Learning Activities

Supporting Thinking in Every Classroom

RALPH PIROZZO

© 2024 Ralph Pirozzo

This work is copyright. Apart from any fair dealings for the purposes of private study, research, criticism or review, or as permitted under the Copyright Act, no part may be reproduced, transmitted, stored, communicated or recorded by any process without written permission. Enquiries should be made to the publisher.

The reproducible pages in this book are available to download at www.ambapress.com.au or www.pli.com.au

Published in 2024 by Amba Press, Melbourne, Australia.
www.ambapress.com.au

Previously published in 2006 by Hawker Brownlow Education.
This edition replaces all previous editions.

Book design: Carmen Dugan
Cover design: Luke Harris

ISBN: 9781923215023 (pbk)
ISBN: 9781923215030 (ebk)

A catalogue record for this book is available from the National Library of Australia.

Contents

Introduction to cooperative learning 5

Activity 1: Design, build and test your own hot air balloon 11

Activity 2: Discover creative uses for regular objects 13

Activity 3: Discovering me! 14

Activity 4: Political contest 16

Activity 5: What is this thing called gravity? 17

Activity 6: Working with Venn diagrams 19

Activity 7: 'Hooking' children into writing (a four-stage approach) 21

Activity 8: Build a pyramid with styrofoam balls 22

Activity 9: Approximating the value of π 24

Activity 10: How entrepreneurial are you? 26

Activity 11: Deciding on a new law 28

Activity 12: How resourceful are you? 29

Activity 13: Interview your favourite author/actor/sportsperson 31

Activity 14: Elect the first governor of a space colony 32

Activity 15: Finding the first chief executive of the Australian space industry 33

Activity 16: Creating a marketing campaign for your school 34

Activity 17: Design an ad for an important person 35

Activity 18: How can we prevent soil erosion? 36

Activity 19: Developing a concept: surface area 38

Activity 20: How to deal with conflict? 40

Activity 21: Preparing yourself for a role 41

Activity 22: Building empathy! 42

Activity 23: Why do some objects float and other sink? 43

Activity 24: Which are your 'preferred' learning styles? 44

Activity 25: The tea bag 'experiment' 45

Activity 26: What does a scientist look and think like? 47

Activity 27: How can Brazil improve honey production? 48

    A true story: The bee that got away 49

Activity 28: Creating your own food web 50
    Creating your own food web 52
    Food web including the long-necked tortoise 53
Activity 29: Learning about diseases 54
Activity 30: How can we get children to stop smoking? 55
Activity 31: Will the Internet change the way you relate with others? 56
Activity 32: I want it all and I want it now! 57
Activity 33: What will Australia be like in the year 2020? 58
Activity 34: How should we deal with refugees? 61
Activity 35: Battlefield of the future! 64
Activity 36: When families drift apart what impact does this have on the children? 67
Activity 37: Dealing with bullying! 68
Activity 38: Genetically modified foods ... who can you believe? 69
    Who can you believe? 70
Activity 39: Introducing magnetism to young children 75
Activity 40: Should scientists be allowed to create a new 'organism'? 77
Activity 41: Why would you want to go to the North Pole? 78
    Caroline Hamilton and the ice girls 79
Activity 42: How is the Internet impacting on you? 80
Activity 43: Should fathers take paternity leave? 82
Activity 44: The 'magical' potato 83
Activity 45: Design, build and test your own rocket 85
Activity 46: Testing foods (for young children) 87
    Follow up activities 88
Activity 47: Design, build and test your own bridge 89
Activity 48: Saving the panda 91
Activity 49: What will you do? 93
Activity 50: did the US government do the 'right' thing by returning Elian Gonzales to his father in Cuba? 94
    Elian Gonzales 95
Thinking tools 96

Introduction to cooperative learning

This book has been designed specifically to engage and motivate primary and secondary school students to think 'outside' the box, to create new ideas and to have fun while learning.

These activities have been based on the following underlying principles:
- Children need to be involved in activities that are engaging, relevant and exciting
- Children should have the opportunity to choose various thinking tools to complete and to present the required tasks (the relevant thinking tools can be found at the back of this book).

These activities can be incorporated into the 48-grid matrix which integrates Bloom's Taxonomy and Gardner's Multiple Intelligences. In this way, we will provide for the thinking skills and the learning styles of our students.
It is anticipated that the children will be encouraged to work in groups and to present their ideas through their 'preferred' intelligences.

What is cooperative learning?

Cooperative learning is an instructional strategy in which small groups of students work together to achieve a common goal. In doing so, they maximise their own, and each other's, learning.

Why use cooperative learning?

The roots of cooperative learning can be traced to John Dewey who emphasised that education should be used as a vehicle for teaching citizens to live cooperatively in a social democracy.
More recently, studies conducted by Johnson and Johnson (1989) and Slavin (1983) have found that cooperative learning is superior to more traditional forms of instruction on critical thinking, self-esteem and racial/ethnic relations.

The research base supporting the use of cooperative learning shows that it leads to:
- increased student achievement
- improved inter-group relations
- increased self-esteem
- better working relations with all types of people.

A further reason for using cooperative learning in the classroom is the growing realisation that to survive and to thrive in the Information Age with its associated ever-changing data combined with rapidly changing systems, our students will require critical thinking and collaborative skills (Gibbs, 2001).

It has become very clear that the schools that were organised to serve the Industrial Age, where people worked on individualised and repetitive tasks without much influence over the end-product or service, no longer serve the needs of our present student population.

What makes cooperative learning so successful?

Instinctively, we have always known that students learn more by being active learners rather than simply watching and listening to their teachers. In other words, we learn best by doing!

Researchers investigating why cooperative learning is so effective have suggested a wide range of theoretical models. According to Slavin (1995), these fall into two main categories — motivation and cognition.

Motivation for learning

Motivational perspectives on cooperative learning focus primarily on the reward or goal structure under which students operate (Slavin, 1993). Deutsch (1949) and Johnson & Johnson (1993) have identified three goal structures. This means that there are three basic ways that students can interact in the classroom. They can compete with each other, they can work on their own or they can cooperate with each other.

Competitive learning

In competitive learning, students work against each other to achieve a goal that only a few can attain. In competition, there is a negative interdependence meaning that students can obtain their goals if and only if other students in the class fail to obtain their goals (Johnson & Johnson, 1989). An interpersonal, competitive situation is characterised by negative goal interdependence where one person wins and the others lose. Examples of competitive learning include activities such as a spelling bee or finding the answer to a maths problem.

Individual learning

In individual learning situations, students work alone to accomplish their own goals. Therefore, students are independent of each other and their work is evaluated based on an established criteria. Students perceive that their success is not affected by the achievements or failure of others students (Deutsch, 1962).

Cooperative learning

From a motivational perspective Johnson & Johnson (1989) and Slavin (1983) argue that cooperative learning creates a situation in which the only way group members can attain their own personal goals is if the group is successful. Therefore, to meet their personal goals, group members must help their classmates and encourage their group members to exert maximum effort. In other words, rewarding groups based on group performance creates an interpersonal reward structure in which group members will give or withhold social reinforcers (such as praise and encouragement) in response to group mates' task-related efforts (Slavin, 1983).

Cognitive learning

Whereas motivational theories emphasise the degree to which cooperative goals change students' incentives to do academic work, cognitive theories emphasise the effects of working together. There are two major categories of cognitive theories: developmental theories and cognitive elaboration theories.

Developmental theories

The fundamental assumption of developmental theories is that interaction among children whilst working on appropriate tasks increases their mastery of critical concepts. Vygotsky (1978) describes the influence of collaborative activity on learning as follows: 'Functions are first formed in the collective in the form of relations among children and then become mental functions for the individual.' In his view, collaborative activity among children promotes growth because children of similar ages are likely to be operating within one another's proximal zones of development.

Vygotsky defines the zone of proximal development as 'the distance between the actual developmental level as determined by independent problem solving, and the level of potential development as determined through problem solving under adult guidance or in collaboration with more capable peers'.

According to Vygotsky, instruction in the zone of proximal development awakens and puts in motion an entire series of internal processes of development. At first, these processes are possible only by interacting with those surrounding the child and in collaboration with companions. Then, in the internal course of development these processes eventually become the internal property of the child (Wertsch, 1985).

Similarly, Piaget (1926) held that social-arbitrary knowledge (language, values, rules, morality and symbol systems such as reading and mathematics) can be learned only in interaction with others.

More recently, Gibbs (2001) pointed out that it is the power of being included and valued by peers that actually motivates students to participate in their own learning. In particular, Gibbs believes that positive expectations

and support from ones' peers is crucial in students becoming excited about their own learning.

Cognitive elaboration theories

Research in cognitive psychology has found that if information is to be retained in memory, the learner must engage in some sort of cognitive re-structuring, or elaboration of the material (Wittrock, 1978). For example, writing a summary of a lecture is a better study aid than simply taking notes because the summary requires the student to reorganise the material and sort out what is important in it (Brown, Bransford, Ferrara and Campione, 1983).

One of the most effective means of elaboration is explaining the material to someone else. For example, Devin-Sheehan, Feldman and Allen (1976) found that both the tutor and the protégé benefit from peer tutoring. More recently, Dansereau (1988) found that college students working on cooperative scripts learned technical material better than students working alone. This mirrors the findings of Webb (1985) who discovered that the students who gained the most from cooperative activities were those who provided elaborated explanations to others.

Summary

The research undeniably supports the notion that cooperative learning leads to increased student achievement and that it will prepare students for an economy that requires critical thinking and collaborative skills. However, it should also be stressed that students in the real-world will face situations where all three patterns (competitive, individualistic and cooperative) will operate. Therefore, it is important that they should learn to interact effectively in each of these situations.

For example, Kagan (1994) does not advocate exclusively the use of cooperative learning methods, rather a healthy balance of competitive, individualistic and cooperative classroom structures to prepare students for the full range of social situations they are likely to encounter outside the classroom. Kagan argues that it is hard to imagine a job today that does not involve some co-operation with other individuals and that lack of interpersonal skills is likely to lead many individuals to lose their jobs.

Another powerful reason why students should have the opportunity to work both cooperatively and individually is based on Gardner's theory of Multiple Intelligences (1999). Children need opportunities to develop both their interpersonal-social intelligence and their intrapersonal-intuitive intelligence. This will help them to work with and understand others.

Therefore, given the reality of the job market and the fact that students learn differently, schools need to include both cooperative and individual learning experiences to enable students to develop their full potential.

References

Brown, A., Bransford, J., Ferrara, R., and Campione, J. 1983, Learning, remembering, and understanding in J. Flavell and E. M. Markman (eds.), Handbook of child psychology (4th ed., Vol. 3). New York: John Wiley.

Dansereau, D. F. 1988, Cooperative learning strategies in C. E. Weinstein, E. T. Goetz, and P. A. Alexander (eds.), Learning and study strategies: Issues in assessment, instruction, and evaluation. Orlando, FL: Academic Press.

Deutsch, M. 1949, A theory of cooperation and competition. Human Relations, 2, pp 129-152.

Deutsch, M. 1962, Cooperation and trust: Some theoretical notes in M. R. Jones (ed.), Nebraska symposium on motivation, 275-319. Lincoln, NE: University of Nebraska Press,.

Devin-Sheehan, L., Feldman, R., and Allen, V. 1976, Research on children tutoring children: A critical review. Review of Educational Research, 46 (3), 355-385.

Gardner, H. 1999, Frames of Mind, London: Fontana Press.

Gibbs, J. 2001, TRIBES: A New Way of Learning and Being Together. CenterSource Systems: Windsor, California.

Johnson, D. W. and Johnson, R. T. 1989, Cooperation and Competition: Theory and Research. Edina, Minn: Interaction Book.

Johnson, D. W., Johnson, R. T., and Holubec, E. J. 1993 Cooperation in the Classroom (6th ed.). Edina, Maine: Interaction Book Company.

Kagan, S. 1994, Cooperative Learning. Resources for Teachers, Inc. San Clemente, California.

Piaget, J. 1926, The language and thought of the child. New York: Harcourt, Brace.

Slavin, R. E. 1995, Cooperative learning (2nd ed.). Needham Heights, MA: Allyn and Bacon.

Slavin, R. E. 1993, Cooperative learning and achievement: An empirically-based theory. Paper presented at the annual meeting of the American Educational Research Association, Atlanta.

Slavin, R. E. 1983, Cooperative learning. New York: Longman.

Vygotsky, L. S. 1978, Mind in Society (ed. M. Cole, V. John-Steiner, S. Scribner and E. Souberman). Cambridge, MA: Harvard University Press.

Webb, N. 1985, Student interaction and learning in small groups: A research summary in R. E. Slavin, S. Sharan, S. Kagan, R. Hertz-Lazarowitz, C. Webb, and R. Schmuck (eds.), Learning to cooperate, cooperating to learn. New York: Plenum.

Wertsch, J. V. 1985, Vytosky and the Social Formation of Mind. Cambridge, MA: Harvard University Press.

Wittrock, M. C. 1978, The cognitive movement in instruction. Educational Psychologist, 13, 15-19.

Activity 1: Design, build and test your own hot air balloon

For this activity you will need the following:
- one large plastic bag (72 litres)
- two small styrofoam cups
- a pair of scissors
- masking tape
- four pieces of smooth string (each piece should be 50 cm long)
- hair dryer (ensure that the hair dryer is used by an adult)
- *TAP* technique (page 108)

Learning activities

- Working in groups of four students, use *TAP* to discover the most creative ways that you can use these objects to build and test your hot air balloon.

- Next, using your designs from the *TAP* technique actually build and test your hot air balloon.

- Did it work? If so, why did the hot air balloon 'go up' in the air?

- Predict what would happen to your balloon if you were to use:

    a) a smaller or larger bag

    b) a bag that is made of heavier material or lighter material

    c) a 'weaker' or 'stronger' air dryer

    d) a hair dryer that produces only cold air

- You live in a two-storey house. On an extremely hot day, where would you find the coolest part of your house to sleep? Why?

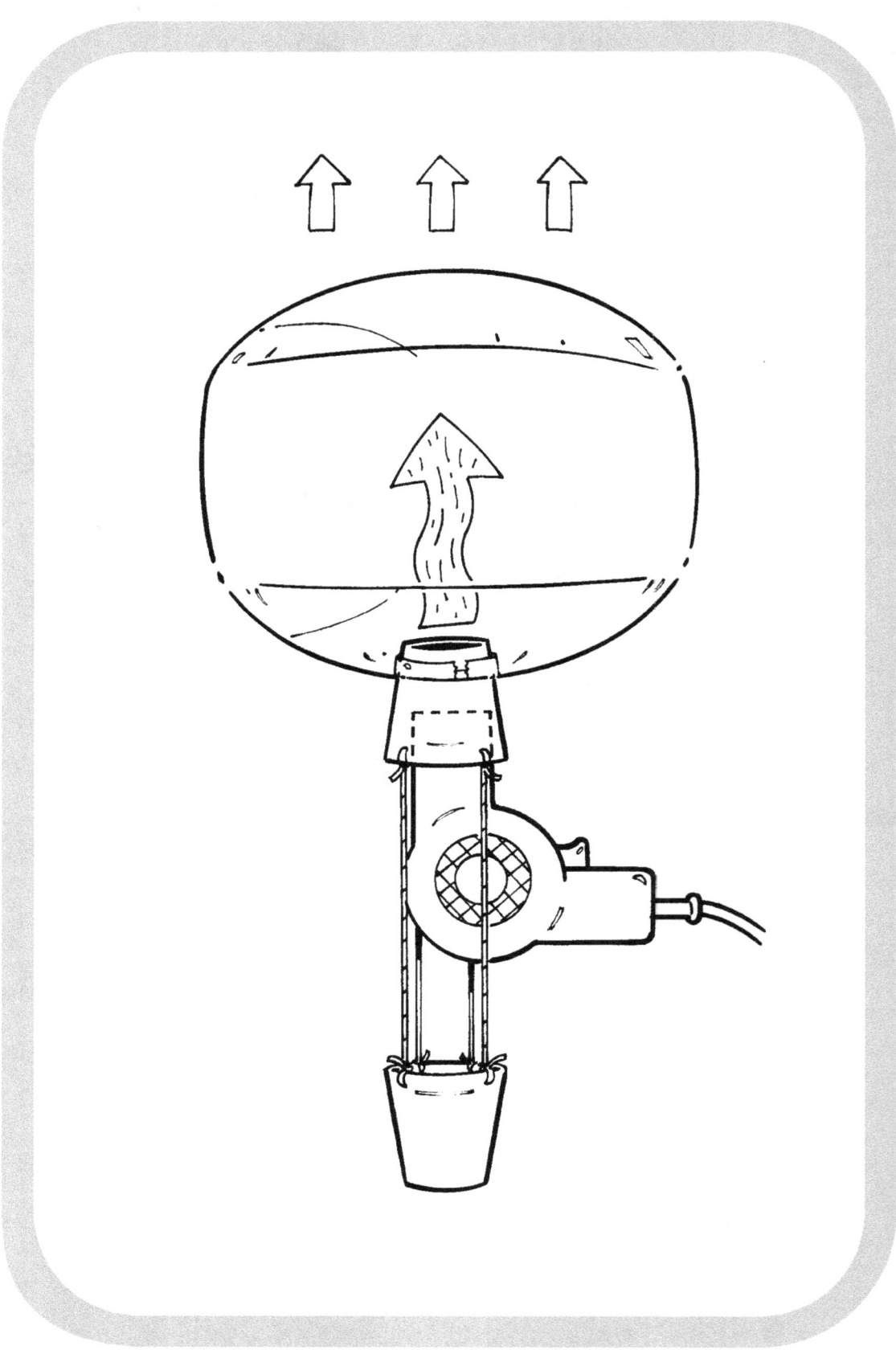

Activity 2: Discover creative uses for regular objects

For this activity you will need the following:
- a pen/pencil
- a styrofoam cup
- an old newspaper
- an old telephone book
- masking tape
- a pair of scissors
- *TAP* technique (page 108)
- *WINCE* strategy (page 113)
- *LDC* (page 100)

Learning activities

- Working in groups of four students, discover the most creative ways that you can use these objects or create something from them by using *TAP* and then mind map all the possibilities.

- Given the fact that you have limited amount of time and materials, choose only three items from your list to be built. How did your group decide on which items to build?

- Now, use the *WINCE* strategy to actually build your 'prototypes'.

- Present your results to the class using a variety of presentations. Use *LDC* to receive feedback from the other students.

- What did you learn by doing this activity?

- How could you improve your 'prototype'?

Activity 3: Discovering me!

In small groups, each person should complete each of the learning activities individually, then discuss their work with their group members. You will also need the following tools:
- *X or Y chart* (pages 115–116)
- *Introducing children to multiple intelligences worksheet* (page 101)
- *TPSS* method (page 110)
- *Thinking tools* (pages 97–116)

Learning activities

- Complete an *X or Y chart* on yourself.

- Complete *Introducing children to multiple intelligences* by following this process:

- Study this page and then place one number, from 1 to 8, in each of the eight grids. Place a 1 in the area that you enjoy working/learning the most and an 8 in the area that you like the least. Continue until you have placed a number in each grid.

- In which grid did you place 1 and in which grid did you place 8?

- Now, create your own 'cluster of intelligences'. To do this, select the three intelligences that you gave a score of 1, 2 and 3. This means that you often solve problems and deal with issues using a number of intelligences rather than just one.

- Use *TPSS* method and discuss the results with your group.

- Answer each of the following questions:

    a) What activities/sports/hobbies/subject areas/foods do you enjoy most?

    b) Discuss 'why are friends important to me'?

    c) I learn best when my teachers engage me by …

    d) Do you prefer solving problems by yourself or by working with other children?

    e) Are you an independent learner or do you need constant directions from your teachers?

f) Do you make decisions 'on the spot' or do you carefully analyse all the choices available to you?

g) Do you prefer learning by using Thinking clouds or concept maps? Why?

h) Look at the Thinking tools. Which of these thinking tools will be most useful to you?

i) Based on what you know about yourself, predict the most suitable job for you. Share this with your group. Do they agree with you?

- Now, complete the following statement: If I were the Prime Minister of Australia/Principal of my School/Mayor of my Town, I would change …

Activity 4: Political contest

For this activity students need to form groups of four. One student will be the group's nominee for president of the student council, one student is the campaign manager and the other two students are administrative campaign supporters. Remember, when on the campaign trail the nominee may be the most obvious spokesperson, but their ideas and beliefs represent those of their whole party or group. You will also need the following tools:
- *X or Y chart* (pages 115–116)
- *BROW* (page 98)
- *LDC* (page 100)
- *TAP* technique (page 108)

Learning activities

- Each group should discuss the strengths of their nominee, consider what people expect of the president of the student council and what the nominee would bring to the role.

- To help the group 'visualise' what the role of president is like, you should complete an *X or Y chart*.

- As a group, use *BROW* to prepare your nominee's speech.

- Each nominee presents their speech then invites the other students in the class to provide their group with feedback by using the *LDC* thinking tool.

- Based on the students' comments and the way each group member 'felt' at the end of the speech, what could the group have done differently to improve the speech? *TAP* may be of some value here.

Activity 5: What is this thing called gravity?

For this activity you will need the following:
- a pen/pencil
- a piece of steel (a nail about 5 cm long)
- a plastic ruler
- a small book
- a feather
- a piece of paper
- an eraser
- a coin
- an apple
- a piece of blue tac
- a paper clip
- a small piece of wood
- a small stone
- a piece of chalk
- a piece of cardboard
- *PSDR* method (page 104)

Learning activities

- Working in groups of four students, use the *PSDR* method to predict which of the above objects will land on the floor first when dropped from the same height.

- Carry out this experiment by actually dropping each of the objects from the same height. Use a watch to find out how many seconds each object takes to hit the ground.

- Graph your results.

- Based on your graph which of these objects hit the floor first? How do your results compare with the rest of the class?

- Can you now explain what 'gravity' is to your group?

- Research what Galileo found when he dropped objects of various mass off the Leaning Tower of Pisa.

- Find out what is the value of one Earth's gravity or '1 G'.

- What would happen to life as we know it, if there was no gravity on Earth?

- Is it possible to create an anti-gravity device? Of what value would this device be to:

    a) a plane whilst taking off?

    b) a semitrailer starting to move again having stopped at a stop light?

    c) you going home on your bike along a very steep road?

- What is your weight on Earth?
    - Why is the Moon's gravity only about 1/6 that of the Earth's?
    - What would you weigh on the surface of the Moon?
    - Would your mass change as you go from Earth to the Moon? Explain.
    - How does gravity impact on you whilst skate boarding?

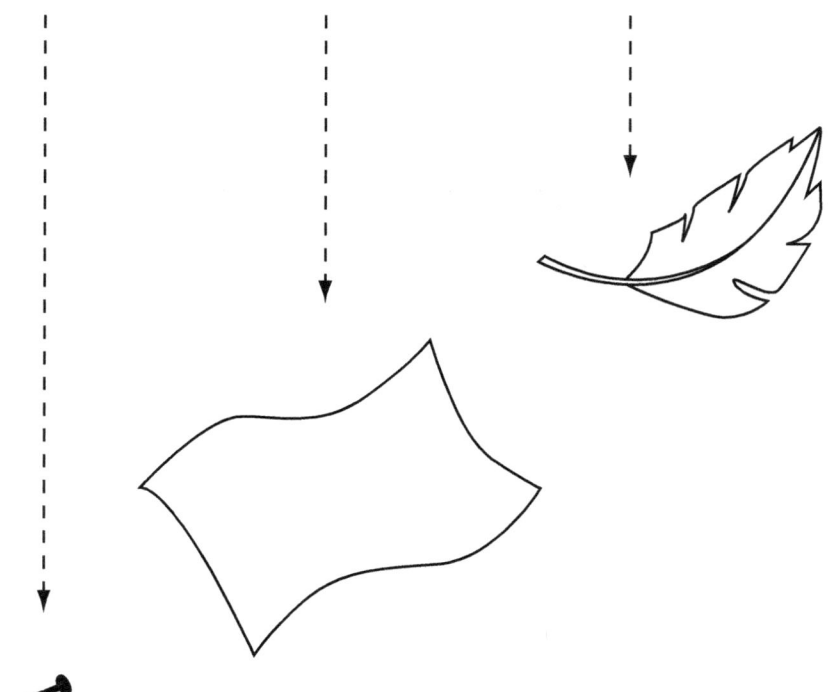

Activity 6: Working with Venn diagrams

Before this activity begins each student will need to:
- find a partner to work with
- collect a copy of, or draw, a *Venn diagram* (page 112)
- familiarise themselves with *Jigsaw* technique (page 102)
- choose one of the following topics, or make up their own and have it approved by the teacher:

  - Telephone vs. mobile phones
  - Day vs. night
  - Winter vs. summer
  - Evil vs. good
  - Democracy vs. dictatorship
  - Leader vs. follower
  - Friend vs. enemy
  - Old vs. new
  - Dishonest vs. honest
  - Dogs vs. cats
  - Acids vs. bases
  - Renewable resources vs. non-renewable resources

Learning activities

- With your partner, use books and the Internet to research your pair's topic.

- Summarise one of the topic's subjects – e.g. renewable resources – on the left side of the *Venn diagram* (use one colour) and the characteristics of the other subject – e.g. non-renewable resources – on the right side of the *Venn diagram* (use a different colour).

- Summarise the characteristics that are common to both subjects – e.g. renewable resources and non – renewable resources in the centre of the *Venn diagram* (use a third colour).

- Once you have completed the *Venn diagram* your teacher will divide the class using the *Jigsaw* technique. Share your findings using the *Venn diagram* within the new group, then return to your partner and teach them what you have learned.

- Now, individually reflect on the value of the *Venn diagram* as a thinking tool by answering the following questions:

  a) Did the *Venn diagram* help you to learn about the topic that you were studying? Explain your answer.

  b) Three different colours were used. Why did we do this?

  c) When will you be able to use this thinking tool again? Share your ideas with your partner.

Renewable and non-renewable resources

Renewable resources are those that can be renewed through natural means. For example, we can renew wheat, cotton and timber by planting more of these plants. Similarly, if we need more meat to feed billions of people, then we raise more animals on our farms and feedlots. However, we need to be very careful when we attempt to harvest very large animals like whales.

Whales are an excellent example of a renewable resource. Until the late 1960's, we were killing about 65000 thousands whales every year for their meat and their oil. Whales' oil is used in cosmetics, automatic car transmissions, softening leather, making margarine and detergents. Given the pressure that this was placing on the number of whales, whaling restrictions were imposed.

In addition to imposing whaling restrictions, we can protect whales by using substitute products. In fact, since the 1960's a synthetic sperm oil from the jojoba bean has been developed.

Non-renewable resources

Unlike plants, non-renewable resources cannot be renewed. For example, once petrol is used to run our cars and coal is burned to produce electricity then these fuels are lost forever. In other words, they can not be renewed.

However, we can reduce the impact that we are having on the use of non-renewable resources by using substitutes and by recycling materials. There is no reason why our clothes should not be made of wool instead of nylon and our furniture could be made of wood instead of plastics and steel. In addition we can recycle a range of materials including paper, glass and metals (e.g. aluminium cans).

Activity 7: 'Hooking' children into writing (a four-stage approach)

This activity has been designed specifically to encourage children to write by involving them in a four-stage approach:

Stage 1: Brainstorm (using a *Thinking cloud*) (page 103)

Stage 2: Design, make and appraise

Stage 3: Use *The Rake* (page 109)

Stage 4: Write a letter

Students will need the following materials:
- an old cardboard box
- a roll of string
- old newspapers
- two paper cups
- a large garbage bag

Learning activities

- Students are asked to brainstorm at least ten places anywhere in the world where they might become lost using a mind map. Then, from the information found on the mind map, the children select only one 'place'.

- They now get out their materials, using them all in order to design, make and appraise a new 'place' that will enable them to survive in the area that they are lost.

- Next, the children use *The Rake* to become aware of the things that they touch, smell, taste, see and hear and what they are thinking whilst in their new place.

- Finally, by using the information that they have gathered from *The Rake*, students write to a parent or a friend to tell them how they have survived in their new place.

Activity 8: Build a pyramid with styrofoam balls

Imagine that you are working at a fruit market and the owner asks you to stack oranges in 5 layers in order to form a square pyramid. Students will need:
- to form groups of about four
- orange-sized styrofoam balls
- toothpicks
- paper and pencils
- *TREC* (page 107)
- *TPSS* (page 110)
- *Venn diagram* (page 112)

Learning activities

- How many oranges do you need in order to stack the oranges as requested by the owner? Use *TREC* to estimate the total number of styrofoam balls needed.

- Draw your own pyramid and share it with your group.

- Using the *TPS* strategy, choose the best pyramid to build. What was the criteria on which this pyramid was chosen?

- Now, use toothpicks and styrofoam balls to build your square pyramid.

- How many styrofoam balls did you need? Is this the number that you had estimated by using *TREC*? If the numbers are different, why do you think this is so? Carry out a group discussion.

- Can you now generate a mathematical equation for a square pyramid? The formula that you generate should allow you to calculate the number of balls required at each level of the pyramid.

- Would this formula help you to build a triangular pyramid?

- Build your own triangular pyramid and then develop a mathematical formula that will allow you to calculate the number of balls required at each level of the pyramid.

- Using the *Venn diagram*, compare and contrast the two pyramids.

- Comment on the value to you of having to draw and then to actually build the pyramids. Carry out a class discussion.

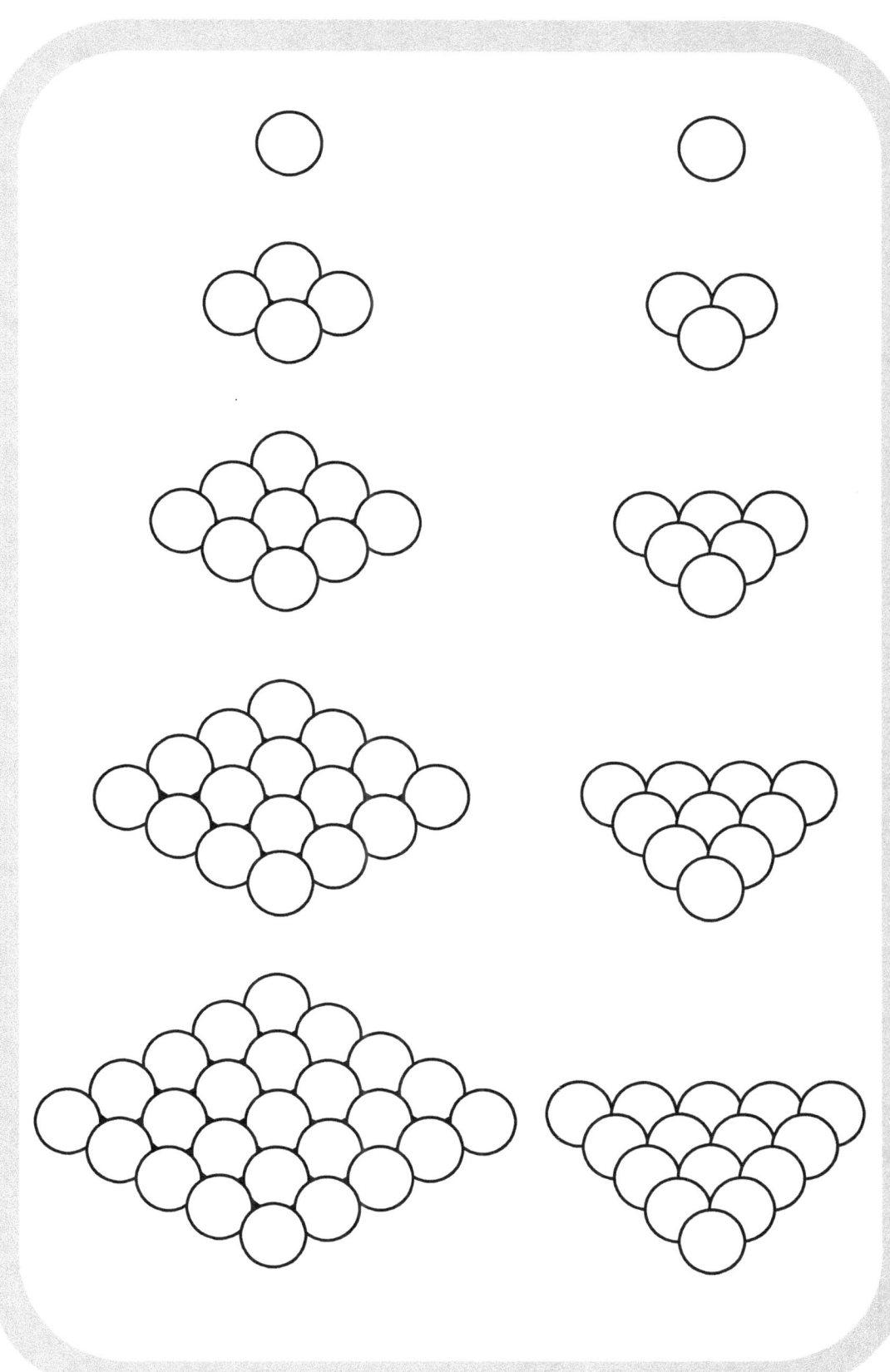

Activity 9: Approximating the value of π

For this activity students will need the following:
- a piece of string approximately 30 cm long
- a piece of string approximately 180 cm long
- a thumbtack
- a pencil and a ruler
- a large piece of butcher's paper
- a pair of scissors
- *TAP* technique (page 108)

Learning activities

- Place a large piece of butcher's paper on the floor.

- Tie one end of the 30 cm piece of string as close as you can to the pointed end of the pencil. Tie the other end of the string to a thumbtack. Measure the distance between the pencil and the thumbtack making sure that this is as close to 25 cm as possible.

- Place the thumbtack in the middle of the butcher's paper and use the pencil at the other end of the string to draw a circle on the paper.

- Working with your group, carefully place the other, longer piece of string over the circle. Make certain that the circle is completely covered by the string.

- Cut the string and measure it.

- You have now found the length of the circumference (C) of the circle. How will you now find the value of π? Use *TAP* and carry out a class discussion.

- One way of finding the value of π is to review the formula for the circumference of a circle: $C=2\pi r$. We have found the value of C, so we need to find the value of π and the radius. Do we already know the value of r? The radius is the length from the middle of the circle to the edge ... the same as the piece of string with the thumbtack and pencil tied to it.

- If $C=2\pi r$ then $\pi = C/2r$. Now, substitute the measurements for C and r and calculate π. How close is the value of your π to either 22/7 or 3.14?

- Draw a circle with a radius of 20 cm and one with a radius of 30 cm.

Calculate the value of π for both circles. What do you notice?

- Class discussion: Is π a constant?

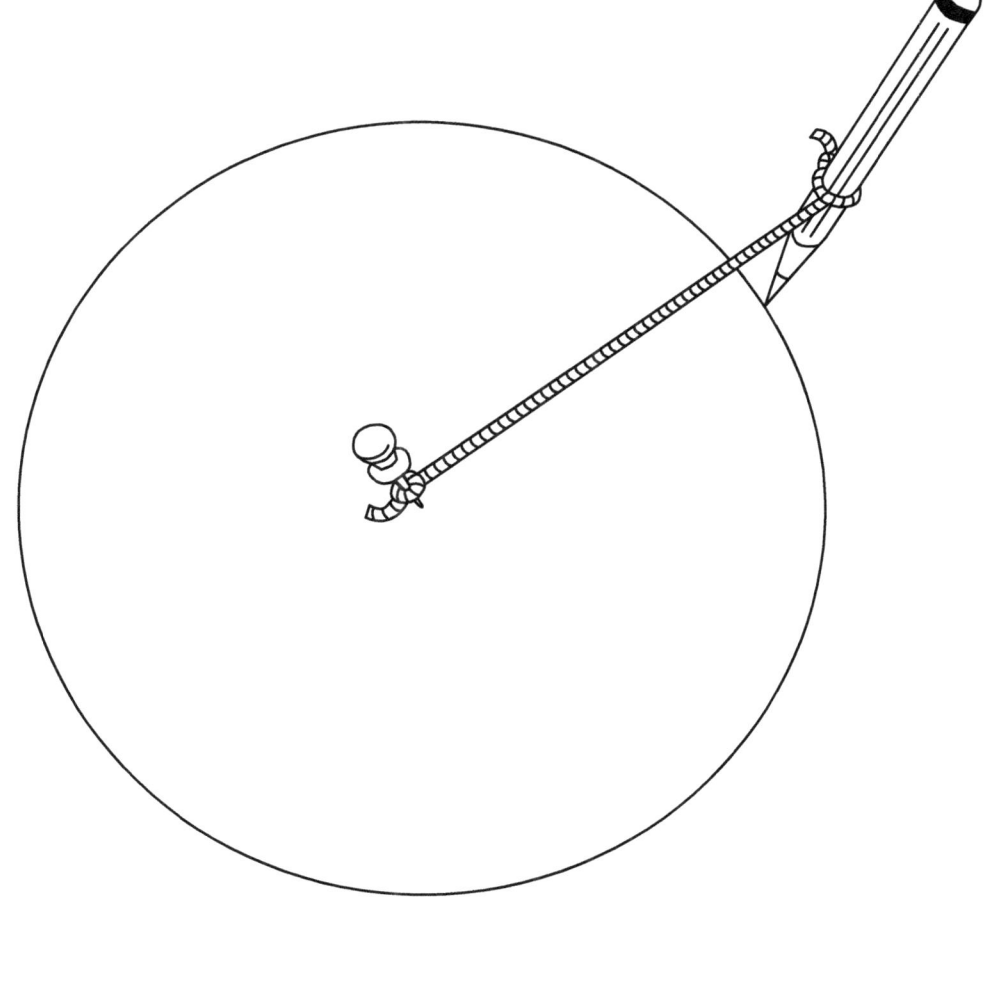

Activity 10: How entrepreneurial are you?

For this activity you will need the following tools:
- *SOWC* analysis (page 106)
- *TREC* (page 107)
- *SCRAM* (page 105)

Learning activities

Pretend that, as part of your Citizenship Education studies, your class has decided to visit Parliament House in Canberra during the last term. There are 30 students in your class and it is assumed that all children will be participating in this excursion. The Principal has given their full support to this trip but cannot offer any financial support from the school so everyone has decided the best option is to begin fundraising. However, due to legal/ethical/heath and safety reasons the Principal has insisted that any activity to raise funds will also need their written support. It is the third week of the school year and your team has been selected to investigate whether or not your class can raise the funds needed to take 30 children to Parliament House. You have been given four weeks to report back to the class with your advice.

- Carry out a *SOWC* analysis.

- Use TREC to calculate how much it will cost to take the following people to your Capital City for a week:

    - 30 students
    - 2 teachers
    - 6 parents
    - 2 bus drivers

In your estimate, please include the cost of:

- hiring the bus for 9 days (it takes 1 day to get to your Capital City)
- food

- soft drinks
- accommodation
- liability insurance
- entry fees to the museums and entertainment parks that you will be visiting whilst in the Capital City
- incidentals

- Based on the *Strengths* that you have identified through the *SOWC* analysis, select only those strategies that you believe will generate funds for your excursion. Analyse these strategies and then list them in order of importance.

- Use *TREC* to estimate the amount of money that each strategy is likely to generate. Now, you are ready to calculate the total funds that you expect to collect by the beginning of final term.

- Will the funds that you are likely to generate from all your entrepreneurial activities cover the anticipated costs of taking your class to visit Parliament House?

- In the event that the answer is no, you may like to use *SCRAM* to see if there are ways of reducing your expenses and increasing your generated income.

- After the four weeks is up, what will your advice be to your teacher and the other 30 students?

Activity 11: Deciding on a new law

To complete the following activities, students will need to form groups that include:
- a principal
- a parent
- a student
- a used-car salesman
- a car-repair shop owner
- a town mayor
- a chairperson

And you will need the following tools:
- *SOWC analysis* (page 106)
- *X, Y or W charts* (pages 114–116)
- *The Rake* (page 109)

Learning activities

By the end of this year, voters will be asked to vote for a new law, which, if passed, will allow children from the age of 12 to buy and drive a car.

• Your job is to decide whether or not you, considering your role in the community, are in favour of this new law. The *SOWC* analysis will be very useful to you.

• Prior to using the *SOWC* analysis, you may like to use the *X, Y or W charts* or *The Rake* to help you in taking on the role given to you.

• Did you find these thinking tools of any value to you?

• Was the *SOWC* analysis of some assistance to you in deciding whether or not you will be in favour of this new law?

• How practical is the *SOWC* analysis in deciding major issues that affect your neighbourhood, city, state or country? Consider the following examples in your response:

    a) Should we set up separate classes for boys and for girls?

    b) Should a safe injection room be established in your suburb?

    c) Should we drill for oil and gas in the Great Barrier Reef?

    d) Should the Prime Minister of Australia say 'Sorry'?

Activity 12: How resourceful are you?

Your parents are driving to a small town to visit your grandparents to celebrate your grandmother's birthday. However, on the way there you run out of petrol and thus your car comes to a sudden stop.

It is now 9.30 a.m. you are in the middle of nowhere, the temperature outside is 38 degrees Celsius, there is no petrol station to be found, shelter is non existent, however there is a good deal of tall grasses nearby. Given that this is a deserted road, there are no cars to be seen. However, you know that there will be a bus coming through at 6.30 p.m.

Your grandparents' town has been hit by a drought for the last four years. This means that vegetables are very expensive in this town. Thus, your parents have purchased the following vegetables to bring to your grandparents:
- lettuces
- broccoli
- cabbages
- cauliflowers.

Your challenge is to devise a number of strategies that will allow you and your parents to survive until 6.30 p.m. using the following strategies:
- *WINCE* strategy (page 113)
- *TAP* technique (page 108)

Learning activities

- Use *WINCE* strategy to help you decide what you are going to do.

- Use *TAP* to brainstorm all the possibilities available to you.

- Analyse all the possibilities available to you and select the three most practical and useful strategies. Why have you chosen these? Justify your choices. Hint: Given that drinking water is going to be very scarce, an excellent strategy would be to use some of the vegetables available. Break them into small parts so that you will have the greatest surface area possible. Add a bunch of tall grasses to the vegetables and then wrap them with a plastic sheet. Place the plastic sheet on top of the bonnet, ensure that the bag is leaning downward and it is facing the sun. Now, cut a small hole in the plastic sheet and place a small cup/bowl right underneath it.

- Did any groups select this strategy to get some drinking water?

- What did the various groups do in relation to shade?

- Present your strategies to your class. The critical issue here is: did you and your parents survive until 6.30 p.m. when the local bus would have rescued you?

- Evaluate this activity. In particular, did it encourage you to brainstorm and to generate a number of very creative ideas and strategies?

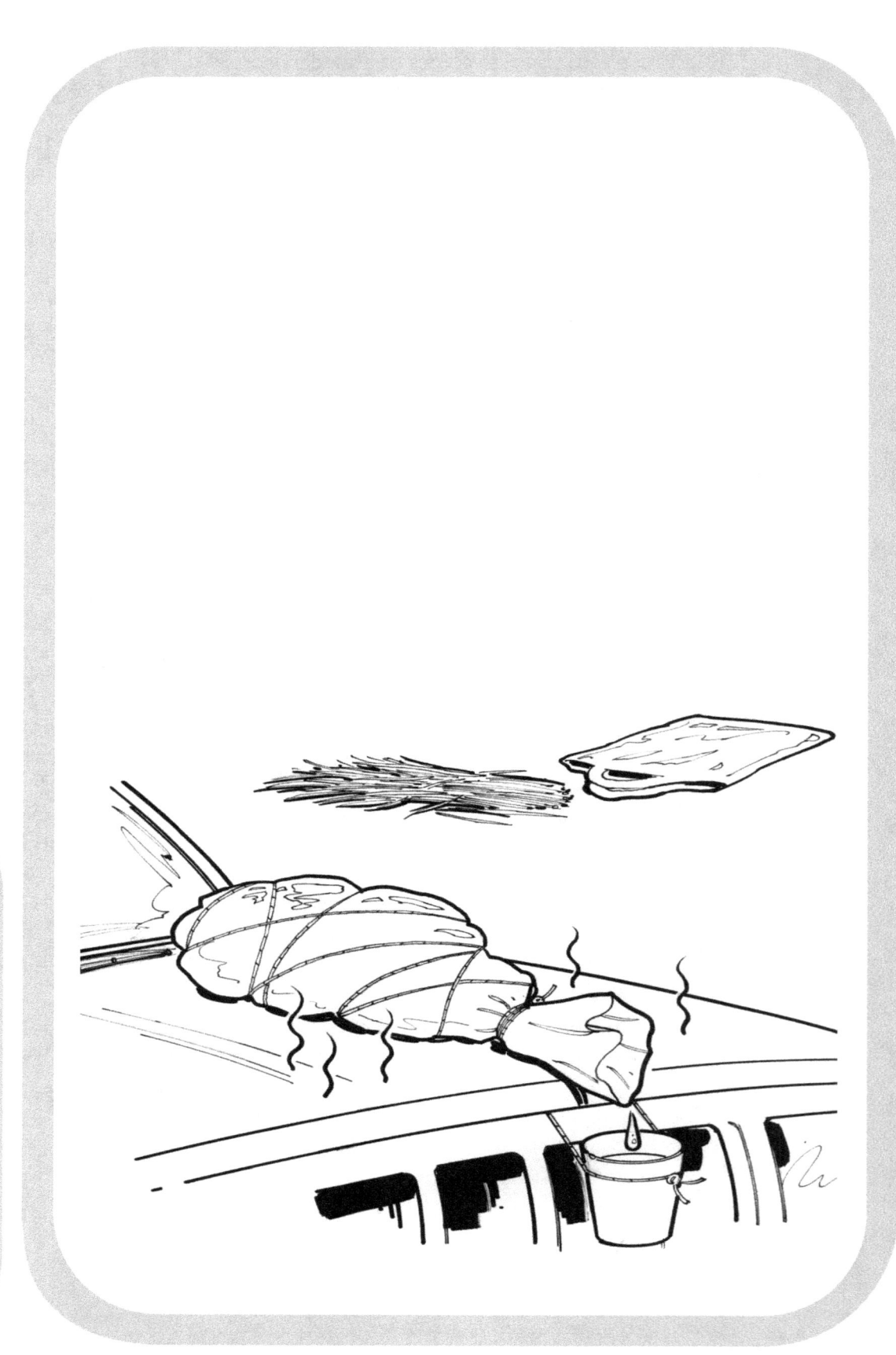

Activity 13: Interview your favourite author/actor/sportsperson

Your favourite celebrity will be visiting your classroom tomorrow. To prepare, form groups of four students, assigning each student one of the following roles:
- Interviewer
- Celebrity
- Journalist for the school or local community newspaper
- Chairperson

This activity uses the following tools:
- *X, Y* and *W charts* (pages 114–116)
- *The Rake* (page 109)
- *LDC* (page 100)

Learning activities

- As a group, use the *X, Y* and *W charts* or *The Rake* to help you prepare your questions.

- Carry out this interview in front of the class and then encourage the other students to provide you feedback using the *LDC* thinking tool.

Activity 14: Elect the first governor of a space colony

For many years, a small group of men and women have been living in a Space Colony. So far, due to its small population there has been no need to elect a governor. However, given a 50% increase in the population during the last twelve months, a meeting has been called to elect the first governor of this colony.

For this activity, the class will need to be divided into three groups. Within these groups, smaller working groups may be formed if desired. You will need the following tools:
- *X, Y and W charts* (pages 114–116)
- *The Rake* (page 109)

Learning activities

- Two class groups will each need to select a 'Candidate' for the position of governor. Then, working as a group, these students will assist the Candidates in preparing themselves for the interview.

- The other third of the class will select an 'Interviewer' and then will assist them in preparing a number of questions that will be put to the candidates.

- Use the *W chart* or *The Rake* to help you in completing this activity.

- Carry out this interview in front of the class.

Activity 15: Finding the first chief executive of the Australian space industry

Australians have shown a good deal of interest in the space industry as shown by the Australian Government passing The Australian Space Activities Act 1998. The first Australian Space Development Conference was held in Sydney on August 24–26, 1990. Basically the space industry in Australia is made up of individuals and organisations that are primarily involved in global positioning, launch services, satellite development, remote sensing, space exploration and telecommunications.

By 2020, Australia has developed a most successful space industry that is now employing thousands of people in a variety of roles providing a number of different services. Your job is to find its first chief executive. This activity uses the following tools:
- *X, Y or W charts* (pages 114–116)
- *The Rake* (page 109)

Learning activities

- Working in groups of four students, your task is to nominate a candidate for the position of chief executive of the Australian Space Industry. Then, the group will assist the candidate to prepare a 3-minute presentation in order to convince the class that they are the best person for this job. What are some of the major characteristics that this person should have? You should research as much information as possible from books, newspapers, magazine and the websites listed below.

- You can choose a variety of presentations including:
    - speech
    - poster
    - debate
    - poem
    - a newspaper/radio/television advertisement
    - song
    - play
    - discussion

- Use the *X, Y or W charts* or *The Rake* to help you in preparing your presentation.

Activity 16: Creating a marketing campaign for your school

Imagine that a new school is being built near yours and is threatening to take all your school's enrolments and potentially close your school. Your team has been selected to create a marketing campaign that will encourage students to enrol at your school rather than at this new school. You can use the following tools:
- *SOWC analysis* (page 106)
- *X, Y* and *W charts* (pages 114–116)
- *The Rake* (page 109)
- *LDC* (page 100)

Learning activities

- Working in groups of four students, prepare an exciting marketing campaign using any of the following:

    - Displays
    - Posters
    - Debates
    - Interviews
    - Newspapers, Radio and Television Advertisements
    - Others
    - Brochures
    - Songs
    - Short Stories
    - Reports

- Use the *SOWC* analysis and *X, Y* and *W charts* or *The Rake* to help you in preparing your marketing campaign.

- Present your marketing campaign to the rest of the class and use the *LDC* to receive their feedback.

Activity 17: Design an ad for an important person

This is a group activity for three to four students; however, each student will need to bring their own ideas to the group and collaborate on the end product. It might help if everyone brings in a newspaper or online job ad for the group to refer to and discuss. This activity uses the following tools:
- *BROW* (page 98)
- *X, Y* and *W charts* (pages 114–116)
- *The Rake* (page 109)

Learning activities

- Your group has been invited to write an employment advertisement for any of the following persons/positions listed below:

    - Friend
    - Parent
    - Grandparent
    - Driver
    - Uncle/Aunt
    - Teacher
    - Principal
    - Coach
    - Dentist
    - Doctor
    - Engineer
    - Actor
    - Sportsperson
    - Politician
    - Religious Person
    - Artist
    - Builder
    - Farmer
    - Mechanic
    - Others

- Which person/position have you selected? Why?

- Share six main characteristics of this person/position with your group.

- Use the *BROW* and *X, Y* and *W charts* or *The Rake* to prepare your advertisement.

- Present your advertisement to your class.

- Evaluate how successful your advertisement will be. In other words, will it attract the best candidate for the job?

Activity 18: How can we prevent soil erosion?

For this activity you will need the following:
- old cardboard boxes
- a pair of scissors
- sticky tape
- a ruler
- a bucket of topsoil
- a bucket of grass clippings or hay
- paper or plastic cups
- 2 bowls

Learning activities

- Using the old cardboard boxes, make two identical boxes with the following dimensions: Length 25 cm x Width 25 cm x Depth 5 cm

- Label one Box A and the other Box B

- Fill Box A with topsoil only.

- Fill Box B with the same amount of topsoil used in Box A. Then, add a layer of grass clippings or hay on top of the soil. Gently pack the grass clippings or hay.

- Place Box A and Box B on a slight slant of about 15 degrees and gently pour the same amount of water, using a cup measuring about 200 ml, to the top of each box.

- Collect the run off from Box A and Box B in two similar bowls.

- Complete the following:

    a) Which bowl has the most amount of water in it?

    b) Which bowl has the most amount of topsoil in it?

    c) Now summarise what you have learned. In other words what must we do to prevent soil from being washed into creeks, rivers, lakes and oceans?

- Based on what you have learned in this experiment, advise the following individuals what they should do to prevent soil erosion:

- A developer who is going to 'chop' 25 acres of land that is presently covered with native grasses and trees, into 100 house lots.

• A home owner who has moved into a brand new house to find that the builder has removed the topsoil thus leaving bare clay.

• A farmer who is planning to harvest their wheat crop and then plough the fields. The farmer knows that a major storm is predicted to hit the area during the next week.

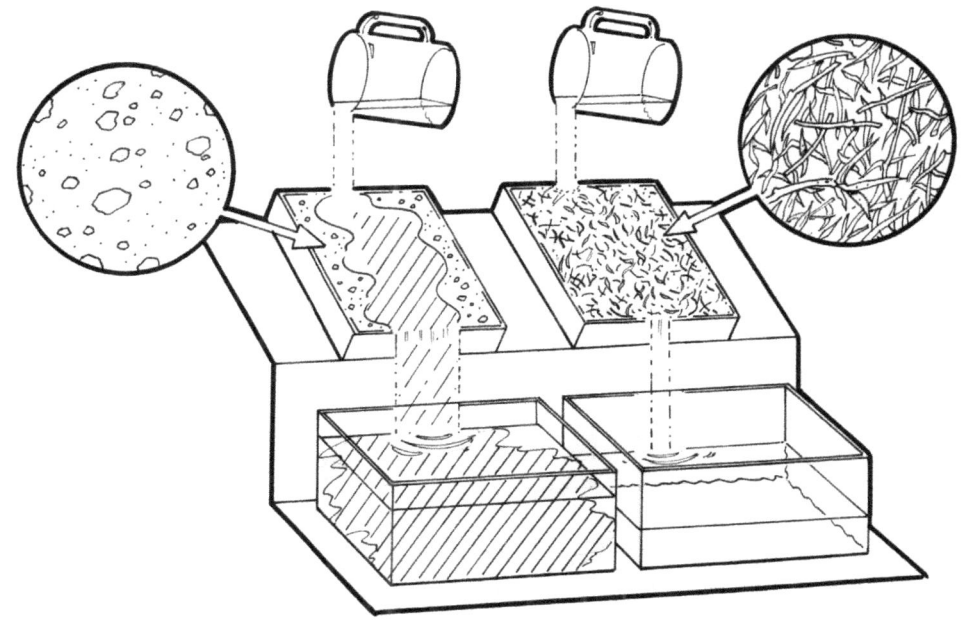

Activity 19: Developing a concept: surface area

The following simple experiment will help to develop an understanding of the concept of surface area and to encourage us to reflect about its impact to our daily lives. This activity uses the following tools:
- 2 small towels (approximately 50 cm x 50 cm)
- *Venn diagram* (page 112)
- *TAP* technique (page 108)

Learning activities

- Take the two small towels and immerse them both in water until they are completely soaked. Remove the towels from the water and hang them as follows:

Towel A – wrap it tightly with some string and then hang it on a line.

Towel B – hang it on the line in the 'normal' way, that is, without wrapping it in any way.

- Use the same hair dryer to dry both A and B. Ensure that the distance that you hold the hair dryer and the angle is the same for A and B. Point your hair dryer on A, for 1 minute, then on B for one minute and continue to do this for ten minutes in total. That means that both A and B will receive a total of five minutes of drying time each.

- Now, check how dry both A and B are by touching them (ensure that you have unwrapped A first). Which of the two towels is drier? Explain why?

- Carry out a *Venn diagram* on A and B to discover their similarities but also how they differ.

- Through the *Venn diagram* you will discover that the only difference between A and B is that A has less surface area exposed to the hot hair coming from the hair dryer. Therefore, A will take longer to dry than B.

- Choose six items listed below and explain how surface area impacts on them.

  - Kidneys
  - Lungs
  - Skin
  - Leaf
  - Hanging and drying clothes
  - Hot air balloons and kites
  - Painting houses
  - Inflating tyres
  - Cleaning chairs, tables and walls
  - Pouring cement
  - Spraying crops (e.g. cotton and wheat)
  - Gluing paper
  - Cutting potatoes and cooking chips
  - Washing and ironing

- Did the experiment with the towels help you to understand how important surface area is in relation to very common human activities such as cutting potatoes in thin slices so that they cook faster?

- You are attending your favourite game in a very large football field. The game has just started when suddenly it starts to rain. It continues to 'pour' for one hour and by now the field is completely soaked and the water is 4 cm deep. It is critical that the game gets underway otherwise the club sponsoring this competition will lose millions of dollars in newspaper, radio and TV advertising fees. Thus, the club is looking for ways to quickly dry the field so that the game can restart as soon as possible. Money is not an issue as the club is extremely wealthy.

- Based on what you know about surface area, what will you suggest to the Club? Use *TAP* to help you to brainstorm many ways of drying the field.

- Select your most promising idea and then advise the club of your decision. Will it work? Will the game be able to continue?

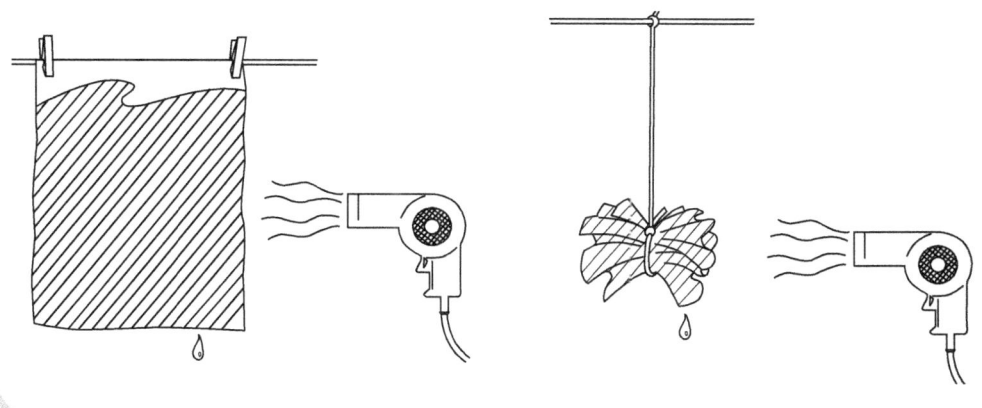

Activity 20:
How to deal with conflict?

Bullying and conflict are common problems kids face at school. Parents and teachers can help out, but it is important for every student to know how to deal with such a situation if it were to arise.

Learning activities

At your school, during morning tea and lunch, a student is constantly teasing, pushing and calling you names in front of your friends. Using the diagram *My Area of Control: Dealing with Conflict* on page 99, answer the following questions:

- What are the things that you can change to improve this very unpleasant situation?
- What are the things that you cannot change?
- Did this activity help you in any way in dealing with this conflict?

Activity 21: Preparing yourself for a role

You are getting ready for an interview/acting role for one of the following occupations listed below:

- Actor
- Animal tamer
- Artist
- Astronaut
- Baker
- Banker
- Bus driver
- Captain
- Clown
- Cook
- Doctor
- Debt collector
- Driver
- Farmer
- Fighter
- Electrician
- Fishing hand
- Jeweller
- Leader
- Musician
- Mechanic
- Nurse
- Painter
- Politician
- Principal
- Salesperson
- Sportsperson
- Teacher

This activity uses the following tools:
- *X, Y or W charts* (pages 114–116)
- *The Rake* (page 109)
- *LDC* (page 100)

Learning activities

- In order to help you in preparing for your interview/role, use the *X, Y or W charts* or *The Rake*.

- Which of these thinking tools did you select? Why?

- Present your interview/role to your class. Will the *LDC* help the other students to give their feedback to you?

Activity 22: Building empathy!

In this activity you will attempt to build empathy for another person. Basically, this means that we need to be able to get 'under the skin' of another individual and really feel what they are going through at a particular time.

You will need the following tools:
- *X, Y or W charts* (pages 114–116)
- *The Rake* (page 109)

Learning activities

- Choose one of the following scenarios.
    - Your grandmother has just won a million dollars.
    - Your best friend has been told that her parents have died in a car accident.
    - Your neighbour's stolen personal possessions have been returned to them.
    - You answer the telephone. The State Manager of a major company is calling to let your brother know that he has been hired for a very important job.
    - Your parents are closing the door of their small business for the last time.
    - Your sister is getting ready to pick up her first car.
    - Complete an *X, Y or W charts* or *The Rake*
  on the person that you have chosen and present this to your class.
    - Did the *X, Y or W charts* or *The Rake* help you to visualise how this individual really felt at that particular moment?

Activity 23: Why do some objects float and other sink?

For this activity, you will need:
- a large bowl (either clear plastic or glass)
- the following fruits and vegetables:

• Apples	• Bananas	• Carrots	• Cucumbers
• Garlic	• Grapes	• Green pepper	• Kiwi fruit
• Mandarins	• Nuts	• Onions	• Oranges
• Potatoes	• Pumpkin	• Tomatoes	• Zucchini

- *PSDR* method (page 104)
- *TAP* technique (page 108)

Learning activities

- Use the *PSDR* method to predict what will happen when these fruits and vegetables are placed in water.

- Which of the above fruits and vegetables float and which sink?

- Can you explain why some fruits and vegetables float whereas others sink?

- Was the *PSDR* method of any value to you?

- Let us suppose that when a potato is placed in water it sinks quickly to the bottom. What can you do to make it float? (You cannot use any weights and/or strings). Brainstorm all possibilities by using *TAP*.

- Now, try your experiment. Does it work?

- Reflect on the outcome of your experiment. If for some reason your experiment did not work, what can you do differently?

Activity 24: Which are your 'preferred' learning styles?

In this activity you are going to discover your 'preferred' learning style or styles. This work is based on the theory of multiple intelligences which argues that you can be smart in at least eight different ways. For this activity you will need a copy of *The engaging wheel* found on page 111.

Learning activities

- Study this page and then place one number, from 1 to 8, in each of the eight grids. Place a 1 in the area that you enjoy working/learning the most and an 8 in the area that you like the least. Continue until you have placed a number in each grid.

- In which grid did you place 1 and in which grid did you place 8?

- Share your preferred intelligence with your group. Do the other students agree with you about yourself?

- Is your preferred intelligence similar to those chosen by other members of your group?

- Collect all the students' data and then graph it. Which 'intelligence' was chosen the most and which was chosen the least?

- Now, create your own 'cluster of intelligences'. To do this, select the three intelligences that you gave a score of 1, 2 and 3. This means that often you solve problems and deal with issues using a number of intelligences rather than just one.

- Evaluate the value of knowing your preferred learning styles to:
    - you
    - your teacher(s)
    - your parents
    - your friends

- Predict what impact your preferred intelligence(s) will have on your future jobs.

Activity 25: The tea bag 'experiment'

You are going to do one of the oldest experiments known, that is, the 'old' tea bag trick and to show what you have learned by completing a *Venn diagram* (page 112).

You will need the following tools:
- *LDC* (page 100)
- *TAP* technique (page 108)

Note: Please make sure that you get your teacher's permission before you light the tea bag and that an adult is present whilst you carry out this activity.

Learning activities

- Look, touch and smell a tea bag. Then, write your observations under 'Before' on the left side of the *Venn diagram*.

- Remove the tea from the bag and light the bag from the top. Observe what happens. Write your observations under 'After' on the right side of the *Venn diagram*.

- Now, look at the left and right side of the *Venn diagram*. Are there any similar characteristics? If yes, move these to the centre of the *Venn diagram*.

- Explain to another student what you have learned by doing this activity.

- Then, join a group of 4–5 students and apply *LDC* to this activity.

- How would you calculate the speed of the 'ashes' as they 'floated' upward? Use *TAP* and share your ideas with your group.

- Did a chemical reaction take place! How could we find out?

Activity 26: What does a scientist look and think like?

Do all scientists look the same? Do they all think the same? What does the average scientist look like? As a class, students will determine the answers to these questions using a range of techniques and drawing from the ideas of a range of people.

You will need the following tools:
- *Venn diagram* (page 112)
- *X, Y or W charts* (pages 114–116)
- *The Rake* (page 109)

Learning activities

- Using the Round Robin strategy, each student writes and draws as much as possible on the topic 'What does a scientist look and think like'.

- After one minute or less, students pass their papers to the person sitting on their left. The students are now invited to add more ideas and designs without repeating what has already been written and drawn. This swapping continues until every student has their original sheet returned to them.

- Interview at least ten different individuals about what they believe a scientist looks and thinks like. Please ensure that you interview your brothers, sisters, parents, neighbours, teachers, shopkeepers and various members of your local community.

- How will you keep a record of these interviews?

- What will you do with this large amount of data that you have gathered? In other words, can you draw some conclusions from this information?

- Use a *Venn diagram* to compare and contrast your view of a 'scientist' with the views expressed by the individuals that you have interviewed?

- Based on your research data, carry out a class discussion titled 'how could scientists improve their public image?'

- Note: in addition to the Round Robin strategy, the *X, Y or W charts* or *The Rake* can also be used for Part 1 of this activity.

Activity 27: How can Brazil improve honey production?

In 1956, the Brazilian government wanted to improve their honey production. This was due to the fact that European bees, which had been brought to Brazil, had not adapted well to their new climate and were not producing much honey. Mr Warwick Kerr, Brazil's top genetics expert was asked to investigate this problem and to advise the government on what should be done to improve the country's honey production. At this time, Mr Kerr was aware of the fact that the African bee is extremely aggressive.

You will need the following tools:
- *The bee that got away*
- *TREC* (page 107)
- *SOWC* analysis (page 106)
- *Venn diagram* (page 112)

Learning activities

- Read *The bee that got away*.

- How far north has the African bee so far travelled in the US?

- How many people have been killed by African bees in the US and South America?

- Estimate the cost to the US alone in trying to stop the African bee from spreading. Use *TREC*.

- Suppose that you were Mr Kerr, given the information that you now have available, what would you recommend to the Brazilian government? The *SOWC* analysis may assist you in making your recommendations.

- Using a *Venn diagram*, compare and contrast your recommendations with the true story *The bee that got away*.

- Carry out a class discussion titled 'What is the message that this story has for us'?

The bee that got away

Due to the fact that in Brazil many people had developed a taste for honey, Brazilian farmers decided to import European honey bees to produce their own honey. Unfortunately, the European honey bees from colder and drier climates such as Spain, Italy and Germany had not adapted well to the hot, wet and humid conditions of Brazil and were producing low quantities of honey. The Brazilian farmers knew that beekeepers in South Africa were getting remarkable honey production from their native honey bees.

In 1956, a well-known geneticist, Warwick Kerr was asked by the Brazilian Agriculture Ministry to obtain some African honey bee queens for experimental purposes with the view of improving Brazil's honey production.

Warwick Kerr then went to Africa and returned to Brazil with 63 African live queens and hundreds of drones of a bee variety known as Apis mellifera scutellata. These African bees were kept in cages in a quarantine area at an agricultural station near Rio Claro. By the end of 1956 only 48 queens were alive.

Kerr had hoped to create a hybrid bee by interbreeding the queens with European drones. It was hoped that the hybrid bee would produce greater quantities of honey and would not be as aggressive as the natural African bee.

In October 1957, according to the story that Warwick Kerr has told many times, a local beekeeper, for some unknown reason, removed the grids over the hives thus releasing 26 queen bees and their colonies into the lush forest near the agricultural station. Kerr thought that the escaped bees would either perish in the wild or mate with European honey bees and eventually lose their aggressive behaviour.

As expected, the African drones quickly crossbred with European queens thus creating a hybrid bee that is well adapted to the Brazilian climate and that produces large quantities of honey. Unfortunately, the hybrid bee developed extreme aggressive characteristics.

By 1974, the hybrid bees had reached Guyana, Venezuela and Panama and by 1986 they had invaded Mexico. Stories of 'killer' bees attacking men, women and children soon created panic in the United States. The US government's reaction was to create a Bee Regulated Zone by setting up thousands of traps and destroying millions of bees.

When this strategy failed to halt the bees, the government proceeded to release thousands of European drones in the hope that they would dilute the aggressive gene of the hybrid bees. Unfortunately, having spent more than 15 million dollars in trying to stop the bees from invading the US, the bees still managed to reach Texas by 1990 and Arizona in 1995. Now, killer bees make up more than 90% of the bee population in many southern US states and they have killed more than 1500 people.

Kerr, was reported in The Australian Magazine (November 27–28, 1999) as saying:

'It is very difficult to control nature […] We should remember and learn from this episode […] If I could do it all again, I swear I'd leave the bees where I found them.'

Prepared by Ralph Pirozzo from material available from the following websites:
http://cals.arizona.edu/pubs/insects.ahb/inf15.html
http://en.wikipedia.org/wiki/Africanixed_bee
http://www.stingshield.com/lebas.htm
http://www.esa.org/ecoservices/poll.case.html

Reference: *The Australian Magazine*, November 27–28, 1999.

Activity 28: Creating your own food web

For this activity students will need:
- Food webs including the long-necked tortoise
- Creating your own food web
- Some knowledge of food chain and food webs

Learning activities

- The students should be given a copy of Food web including the long-necked tortoise so that they can see how the algae (plant) and these animals are inter-related.

- A guest speaker should be invited to talk with the children about environmental issues.

- An excursion to the local pond/creek/lake/river will enable the children to construct their own food webs.

- Next, in order to find out if the students can transfer what they have learned, they are asked to put together their own food web by using Creating your own food web and to answer the following questions:

- What would happen if a farmer were to spray herbicide thus killing all the algae?

- What impact would an increase in the number of tadpoles have on this food web?

- For some reasons, the number of water-snails has increased enormously. Predict what impact this will have on this food web.

- If we were to decrease our consumption of Murray cod what effect will this have?

- Would this food web survive as it is? What is missing?

- Design a new animal that could survive in this food web.

Creating your own food web

Create your own food web by using the following plants and animals:

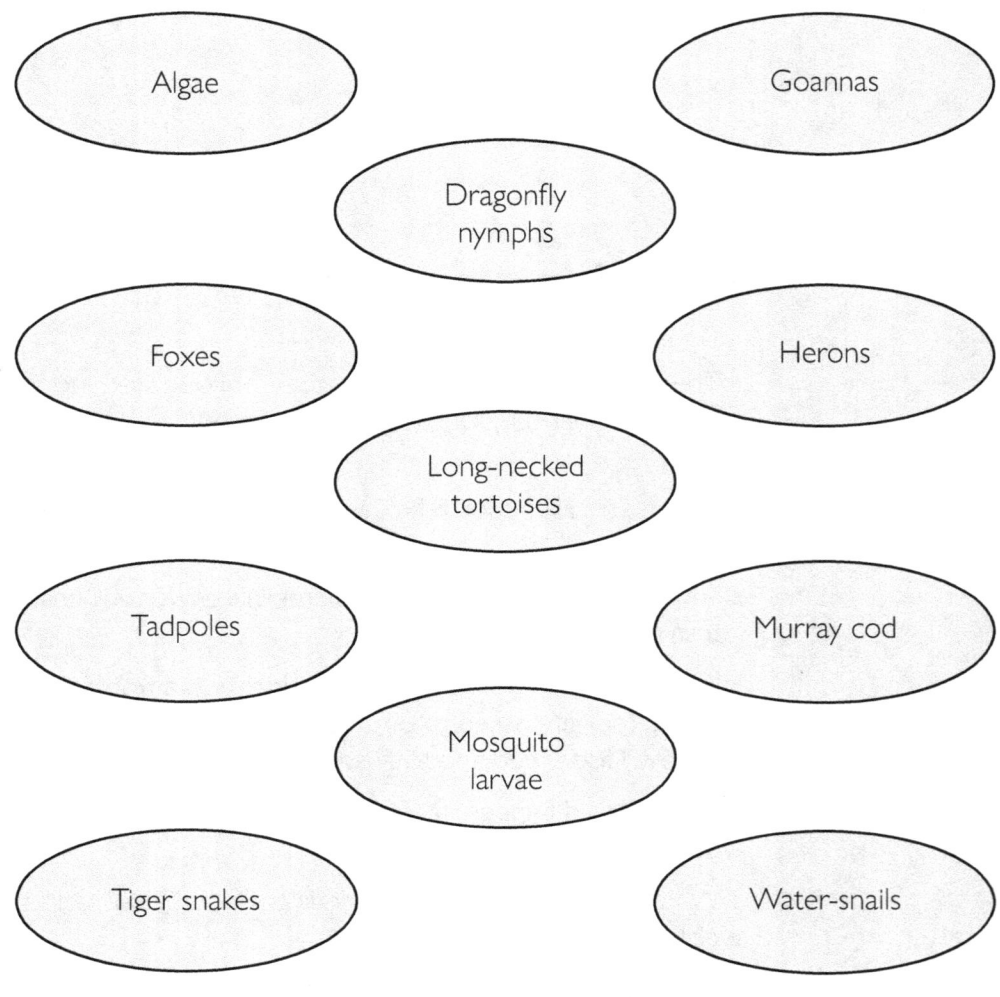

Food web including the long-necked tortoise

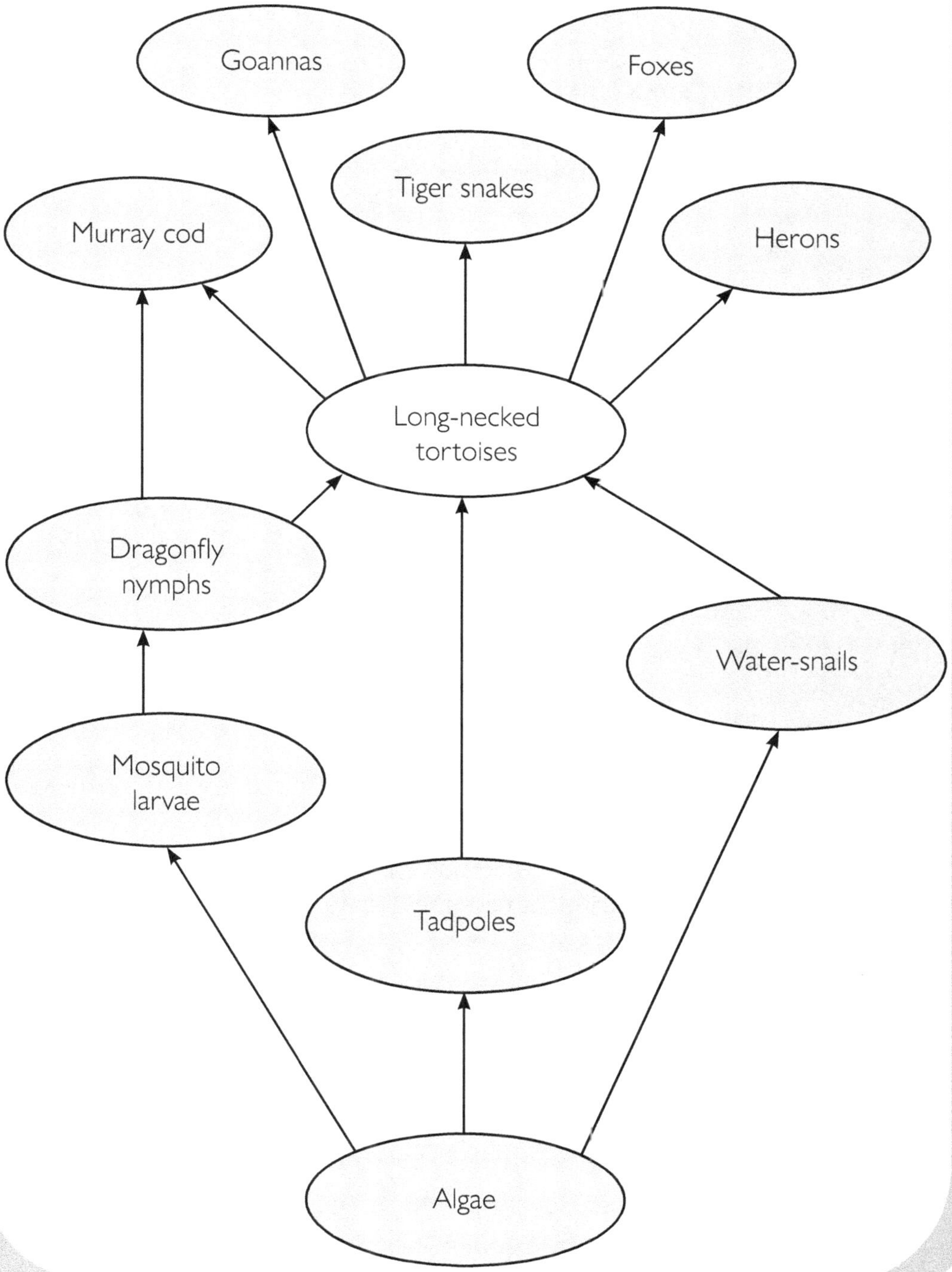

Activity 29: Learning about diseases

From the list provided, choose one disease to further research:

- Anorexia Nervosa
- Bulimia
- Depression
- HIV/AIDS
- Leukaemia
- Peptic ulcers
- Asthma
- Cancer
- Diabetes
- Hepatitis
- Measles
- Smallpox
- Alzheimer's Disease
- Cirrhosis of the liver
- Heart attack
- Kidney failure
- Parkinson's Disease
- Schizophrenia

You will need the following tools:
- *TAP* technique (page 108)
- *LDC* (page 100)
- TREC (page 107)

Learning activities

- Use the *TAP* thinking tool to design a strategy that will enable you to teach all about this disease to your class/a young child/a student with learning difficulties.

- Did your teaching strategy work? In other words, did your class and/or the other students understand what you were trying to teach them? How do you know?

- One way to find out is to invite the class and/or the other students to provide you feedback using the *LDC*.

- How does this disease affect the individuals that have it? What about their families and their communities?

- Use *TREC* estimate the cost of this disease to the individual/family/community?

- Is it likely that advances in gene therapy could in the near future cure the individuals that have the disease that you have chosen?

Activity 30: How can we get children to stop smoking?

Did you know that smoking is the single largest preventable cause of death and disease in Australia killing around 19,000 people every year and costing about 12.7 billion dollars per year. In Tasmania alone the DHHS found that 17% of the population aged between 12 and 17 years were current smokers and that approximately 6300 Tasmanians students were smoking 213,500 cigarettes every week (DHHS, Tasmania, 2001). Based on this figure, we can estimate that more than 120,000 children smoke regularly in Australia. Did you know that 12 to 17 year olds are most at risk of becoming addicted to smoking? Did you know that more than 6000 children die each year in the United States because their parents smoke? Are 12 to 17 year olds ignoring anti-smoking campaigns directed specifically at them? Why?

You will need the following tools:
- *TAP* technique (page 108)
- *LDC* (page 100)
- *WINCE* strategy (page 113)

Learning activities

- Develop a practical campaign that will encourage young children to stop smoking.

- Well, how will you begin? You could use *TAP* to brainstorm all possibilities. Another strategy that could prove to be very valuable to you would be the *WINCE* thinking tool.

- Share your campaign with the rest of the class and encourage the students to comment on your 'creation' by using *LDC*.

- Now, create a campaign to help parents quit smoking. How will this campaign stop parents from smoking in their cars with the windows closed whilst travelling with children?

Activity 31: Will the Internet change the way you relate with others?

Since the birth of the Internet people all over the world can communicate with one another by sending emails which take almost no time at all to reach the other person. In particular, online communities are booming. Individuals can share their ideas with thousands of people in an instant. What will happen if this individual wants to do harm to another person and now has the power to influence others? For example, what will happen when students receive poor marks or voters do not like their Prime Minister?

Presently, a great number of people throughout the world have access to the Internet. This means that people online are now able to express their views directly to their friends, family, teachers, principals, government officials, doctors, shopkeepers and almost anyone else who has access to the Internet. Instead of calling or visiting, people can avoid all direct contact and email others instead.

You will need the following tools:
- *BROW* (page 98)
- *LDC* (page 100)
- *SOWC* analysis (page 106)

Learning activities

- Should parents have the power to prevent their children to have access to some chats rooms? Have a class discussion on this topic.

- If people no longer have the need to visit or talk to others, predict the impact this is likely to have on our ability to communicate with one another? Are we likely to be more friendly towards others or not? Will we need more support from psychologists and psychiatrists? Will our rate of mental illness increase, decrease or stay the same? What do you think?

- Working with another student, interview at least 20 people to find out whether they believe that the ability to express your views online is a good or bad idea.

- How will you present your results to your class? Will the *BROW* strategy be of any value to you?

- Carry out an *LDC* on this issue by involving the entire class.

- Next, use the *SOWC* analysis to predict how the Internet will change the way you are likely to communicate with others in five years from now.

Activity 32: I want it all and I want it now!

Are advertising companies targeting you in the same way that they have been targeting the baby-boomers in order to get you to buy their products?

Baby-boomers is the collective name given to those who were born between 1946 and 1964. They have been dubbed the 'me generation' for their non-stop quest for self-gratification and status seeking. For the baby-boomers binge buying and the abuse of credit cards became a way of life. In doing so, the baby-boomers became known as the splurge generation. Advertising companies have cleverly taken advantage of the baby-boomers' drive to remain young until they die and their quest for status by developing ads like: 'Lord won't you buy me a Mercedes Benz', 'You are worth it' and 'You deserve it'.

Twenty-four hours a day, you are 'bombarded' by radio, TV, newspapers, magazines and road signs that basically encourage you to 'want it all and want it now'.

You will need the following tools:
- X, Y or W charts (page 114–116)
- The Rake (page 109)
- ARC strategy (page 97)
- SOWC analysis (page 106)

Learning activities

- Are labels such as Billabong, Reebok and Ipod important to you and to your friends? Why has Nike decided to use the slogan 'Just do it' in their ads?

- Are your parents baby-boomers? Do they have some of the characteristics that have been mentioned above? Are your spending habits similar to your parents and/or your grandparents?

- Choose the best advertisement that you have seen recently. Use the X, Y or W chart or The Rake to discover how 'clever' advertising people are in convincing you that you MUST buy their goods.

- Use the ARC strategy to become aware of how you react when you see an advertisement for a brand new bike, pair of shoes, new dress, the tastiest food, the most exciting ride, the latest CD or mobile phone and the 'coolest' computer game.

- Now, use the SOWC analysis to predict and then to debate the following topic: What will the impact on the world of 'The Me Generation' be in 10 years from now?

Activity 33: What will Australia be like in the year 2020?

Before you complete this activity, consider how much you know about Australia today? For example:
- What is Australia's present population?
- Does our country have a treaty with our indigenous people?
- How large is Australia in terms of land mass?
- How many states and territories are there?
- How many different ethnic groups are represented in Australia?
- Why did so many migrants decide to come to Australia?
- Who are Australia's major trading partners?
- Which goods and services does Australia export?
- Which goods and services does Australia import?

Learning activities

- Based on your knowledge of Australia today, predict what Australia will be like in the year 2020 and complete the following questions, providing reasons for your responses:

    - Will we have a treaty with our indigenous people?

    - Will we set aside a certain number of seats in Parliament and the Senate for our indigenous people? Do other countries have this type of agreement?

    - What will be our population and ethnic makeup?

    - Will we be fully accepted by other Asian countries?

    - Will we have a Monarchy, Republic or another form of Government?

    - Will we have abolished poverty?

    - Will we be drilling for oil in the Great Barrier Reef?

    - Will we be mining uranium for nuclear purposes?

    - Many nations see Australia as 'The Lucky Country'? Will this continue to be the case in 2020?

    - Will most young couples continue to live with their parents for a long time because they cannot afford to buy their own homes?

    - Will we have in place strict policies to prevent large forests from being cut down?

- Will we have strict laws to ensure that we will reduce water wastage and stop polluting our environment? Will we have desalination plants serving the water needs of every major city?

- The government has refused to sign the Kyoto Protocol which aims at reducing the levels of carbon dioxide (CO_2) emission. Why has Australia decided to do this? In 2005, the government instead strongly promoted The Pacific Partnership which includes Japan, China, India, South Korea, US and Australia. What does this partnership aim to achieve? Have these countries signed any agreements?

- Why did Australia sign a Free Trade Agreement with the US? What impact is this likely to have on our imports and exports? Who will gain most from this agreement, Australia or the US? Why?

- Is Australia likely to be the first country in the world to reduce its dependency on oil by 2020? Will we be driving electric cars?

- Will Australia become the dominant country in the South Pacific?

- Environmental experts predict that global warming will raise sea levels thus making many of the small Pacific Islands uninhabitable. Given the fact that Australia has contributed to climate changes by relying so heavily on fossil fuel, does Australia then have an obligation to resettle these people?

- What will be our relationships with East Timor? Indonesia? Papua New Guinea? China? US? Will the ANZUS Treaty continue to be of any relevance?

- Will Australia followed Canada and change its flag so that it is more representative of its fauna and flora?

- Will Australia have a population of over 30 million people?

- Given that the percentage of the population over 65 years is increasing and will continue to do so for many years, how is the government going to continue to provide basic services such as health, education and welfare? In other words, where is all this money coming from?

- Will we have many terrorist cells operating from this country?

- Is Australia likely to become a leading nation in global technology, solar energy and biotechnology?

- Will Australia become the world's uranium reprocessing centre?

- In 2005, Australia introduced its new Industrial Relations Laws. Some claim that this will lead to unprecedented prosperity whilst others stress that this will lead to the formation of an underclass of workers in this country. Who is right? Research and debate.

- The coal industry is extremely strong in Australia. By 2020 will we abandon our dependency on coal? Will we be relying much more on renewable energy such as wind power?

- What role(s) can you play to ensure that this country continues to be free and prosperous?

Activity 34: How should we deal with refugees?

Christmas Island is an Australian territory located about 2000 km off the north-west coast of Australia. During 2001, hundreds of people arrived at Christmas Island from Indonesia on leaky boats having paid thousands of dollars to people smugglers. In legal terms, once asylum seekers arrive at Christmas Island then they have the right to be granted refugee status in Australia.

You will need the following tools:
- Read *The facts*
- *X, Y or W charts* (pages 114–116)
- *Venn diagram* (page 112)
- *TAP* technique (page 108)

Learning activities

- Discover what has happened to the asylum seekers. Are they still in Nauru?

- What happened to Captain Arne Rinnan?

- What impact did the Tampa crisis have on Australia both at home and abroad?

- Why did the Australian government's popularity rise throughout the crisis?

- How do you explain the fact that whilst TV news polls showed the government receiving huge support, many human rights and religious organisations became deeply concerned about the lack of compassion shown by the government towards the asylum seekers?

- During the federal election that was held soon after the Tampa incident, the Prime Minister regularly stated that "we decide who come into this country and the circumstances in which they come". What impact did this have on the election?

- What were the reasons that the Australian Government gave in refusing the Tampa from entering Australian waters?

- Has Australia's Pacific Solution worked? How do you know?

- Why did Australia, a country that has welcomed millions of people from every corner of the world, take such radical and drastic steps to deal with the Tampa's asylum seekers?

- Imagine that you are a young Afghani asylum seeker on board the Norwegian vessel Tampa and that you are listening to Captain Arne Rinnan addressing the 438 asylum seekers through a loud speaker. This is what he is saying: "Australia will not allow the Tampa to dock at Christmas Island and soon Australian SAS troops will board the Tampa to make sure that we do not dock there".

• Complete the *X, Y* or *W charts* or *The Rake*.

• Use the *Venn diagram* to compare this young Afghani asylum seeker with a child of the same age in your town/suburb/city.

• Write a letter to your friend(s) in Afghanistan using the information that you have gathered from completing the *X, Y* or *W charts* and the *Venn diagram*.

• How should Australia deal with asylum seekers? Use the *TAP* technique to deal with this issue.

• Based on *TAP*, organise a class debate.

The facts:

- At dawn on August 24, 2001 a 20 metre wooden fishing boat, the Palaga, with 438 mainly Afghan asylum seekers on board, became stranded about 140 km north of Christmas Island.

- On August 26, 2001, Rescue Coordination Centre Australia asked all ships in the area to respond to the Palaga's distress. The Tampa, a Norwegian cargo ship, was closest to the area and rescued the asylum seekers.

- According to international law, survivors of a shipwreck are to be taken to the closest port. In this case, Christmas Island was the closest port.

- Even though Captain Arne Rinnan had been directed to the Palaga by an Australian plane, he was told that the asylum seekers were not allowed to disembark on Christmas Island.

- On August 29, 2001 Captain Rinnan declared a state of emergency and entered Australian territorial waters without permission. The Australian government responded by sending 35 SAS commandoes to board the ship, thus preventing it from getting any closer to Christmas Island. The SAS commandoes instructed Captain Rinnan to move his ship back into international waters. The Captain refused on the basis that the Tampa was designed as a cargo ship to house 27 crew not to carry 438 passengers. He pointed out that the ship did not have enough lifeboats, toilets and sleeping facilities. In other words with 438 people on board, the Tampa was unseaworthy.

- The Australian government tried to get Indonesia and Norway to accept the asylum seekers but both refused. Then, Norway reported Australia to the United Nations, the United Nations High Commissioner for Refugees and the International Maritime Organisation for alleged failure to carry out its duties under international law.

- On August 29, 2001 the Prime Minister of Australia introduced the 'Border Protection Bill 2001' which gives the government the power to remove any ship in the territorial waters of Australia and to refuse asylum applications to the people on board the ship. Since then, the Australian government has excised Christmas Island and many other coastal islands from Australia's migration zone. Basically, this means that now asylum seekers have to reach the mainland of Australia in order to apply for refugee status.

- Finally, the asylum seekers from the Tampa were loaded onto the HMAS Manoora and transported to Nauru as part of Australia's 'Pacific Solution'.

Activity 35: Battlefield of the future!

Can you predict how the battlefield will look by the end of the 21st century? In 1999, Stewart and Beal summarised the predictions made by a number of arms experts in relation to the 'likely' future for war. Read these experts' predictions, then gather data from newspapers, the Internet, textbooks and TV documentaries to decide whether their predictions have actually become reality.

You will need the following tools:
- *TREC* (page 107)
- *TAP* technique (page 108)

Predictions Made

IN THE AIR

- The US-led Joint Strike Fighter (JSF) would be the biggest combat aircraft by the year 2020. This would replace the Harrier in the RAF and in the US Marine Corps.

- The American 'killer' Airborne Laser gun would be able to track and destroy Scud missiles.

- Unmanned Aerial Vehicles would perform a variety of roles such as jamming enemy transmission, providing communications links, spotting lasers and knocking out enemy missile sites.

- Robotic aircraft, guided by remote human pilots from base, would engage targets in the air.

- Manned hypersonic bombers would be used as space becomes the ultimate 'high-ground' of war.

ON THE GROUND

- Soldiers would wear helmets with microphones and earphones, night-vision goggles, body armour and they would have their own computers and computer-assisted rifle-grenade launchers.

- In addition, a small screen in front of the soldiers' eyes would enable them to locate their own position and access the latest intelligence. Once an enemy has been spotted, the soldier would simply press a button on their laptop to destroy a 'target'.

ON THE SEA

- Britain, France, Sweden and the USA would build ships able to absorb and dissipate radar waves. This would enable them to stay undetected longer and therefore they would be much more difficult to hit.

- The US Navy would build guided-missile cruisers armed with a modified 'Aegis' radar that would track enemy ballistic missiles in flight and fire the new SM-3 missile to the edge of space.

By 2006, the scenario of the battlefield of the future has been further complicated by our concern with weapons of mass destruction (WMD) including biological and chemical warfare. Biological and chemical warfare are not new, they have been used as weapons since 1346 A.D. when the Tartars conquered Kaffa by catapulting plague-infested bodies into the city. Then, two thousand years ago, the Romans polluted their enemies' water supplies by throwing the corpses of dead animals in the wells. More recently, during the American Civil War, Confederate soldiers shot horses and other farm animals in order to contaminate the Union Forces' water supplies. During World War 11, the Nazi are reported to have gassed more than six million people mainly Jews and on March 20, 1995, the Tokyo subway system was attacked with Sarin nerve gas by cult members of Aun Shinri Kyo or the Supreme Truth.

In particular, biological warfare is seen by some experts as "a poor nation's weapon of mass destruction" because only very small doses of these biological agents such as botulism and anthrax are needed to kill thousands of people. Furthermore, these programs are very hard to detect.

Learning activities

- Study the material that you have gathered and determine which of the experts' predictions have already taken place?

- By relying too much on computers, have soldiers become 'desensitised' to the pain and agony of killing another person? What effect will the reliance on computers have on the number of women in the armed forces?

- How many people died due to poison gas during World War 1? What was the aim of the Geneva Protocol of 1925?

- In August 1945, the US dropped atomic bombs on Hiroshima and Nagasaki. Do the people that live in and around these two Japanese cities continue to suffer the effects of radiation? Given the fact that the US signed the Biological and Toxin Weapons Convention (BWC) in 1972, could they ever use atomic weapons again?

• Japan is accused of dropping flea-infested debris over 11 Chinese cities during WW11. Research the impact that this had on Chinese citizen.

• During the Vietnam War, the Americans destroyed thousands of acres of land by spraying a chemical called Agent Orange. What impact did Agent Orange have on the people that were exposed to it?

• In 1972, a total of 118 countries signed the BWC. What impact has the BWC had in preventing the spread of biological weapons? What happens if a member country is found to be producing biological weapons?

• Did the regime of Saddam Hussein gas his own people in 1988? Why were the Kurds persecuted by his regime? Is Iraq a signatory to the BWC?

• In the future, are we likely to see "killer insects" being developed that have the capacity of hunting down their prey in bunkers and caves and eating humans alive? Can this really happen?

• Will developing countries and terrorists use biological weapons to wage war against rich and powerful countries?

• Use *TREC* to calculate the total amount of money that is now spent yearly on military spending throughout the world?

• If this money were not spent on preparing for war, use *TAP* to discover all the 'things' that we could do with these funds?

• If we were to stop manufacturing arms, what effect would this have on the employment and on the economy of some countries?

• Which countries benefit most from the arms race?

• Are we ready and willing to build a 'war free' world? What do you think? Carry out a class debate on this topic.

References: Stewart, C. *The new canons of war.* The Weekend Australian, page 8, December 11-12, 1999.

Beal, C. *Weaponry that keeps its distance.* The Weekend Australian, page 8, December 11-12, 1999.

Activity 36: When families drift apart what impact does this have on the children?

Undeniably, dealing with the issue of 'families drifting apart' is very difficult and painful for some children. Teachers constantly make decisions whether or not to 'allow' some controversial issues to be discussed in classrooms. Thus, based on the knowledge that you have of your students, you will decide whether or not to involve your children in this activity.

Now, let us begin with the facts. In Australia 54,000 divorces were granted in 2002 (Australian Bureau of Statistics, 2002). From this, we can predict that thousands of children live with one parent, in shared care arrangements and in foster homes.

You will need the following tools:
- *Thinking clouds* (page 103)
- *TAP* technique (page 108)

Learning activities

- With a partner, brainstorm the question 'Why do families break apart?' then use these ideas to create your own *Thinking cloud*.

- Analyse this data and then list the most common or influential factors that contribute to divorce.

- Investigate what can be done to prevent some families from breaking apart.

- Carry out a debate titled: 'When parents drift apart from one another, what effect does this have on the children'?

- What can we do in our classrooms, to empathise with (not pity) children that come from broken families? Use *TAP*.

Activity 37: Dealing with bullying!

The most common issue teachers and students are facing in schools today is bullying. It is important to consider the signs shown both by bullies and those being bullied in order to help deal with the problem.

You will need the following tools:
- *X or Y charts* (pages 115–116)
- *Venn diagram* (page 112)
- *My area of control: dealing with conflict* (page 99)
- *SOWC* analysis (page 106)
- *TREC* (page 107)

Learning activities

- What do we mean when we say that someone is a bully? What are their main characteristics?

- Complete an *X or Y chart* on a bully.

- What are the major characteristics of a victim?

- Complete an *X or Y chart* on a victim.

- Compare and contrast a bully and a victim using a *Venn diagram*.

- Is bullying still taking place at your school today?

- How many incidences have you witnessed when someone was being bullied? Did these incidences occur in the classroom, playground, home, shopping centres, park, highways and/or in others areas?

- Complete the diagram titled *My Area of Control: Dealing with Conflict*.

- Carry out a *SOWC* analysis on the topic titled 'How can we best deal with bullying?'.

- Do we know what happens to children who were labelled as 'bullies' whilst in school as they get older? Is there any available data?

- What about the victims? What happens to them as they leave school and enter the workforce?

- Use *TREC* to calculate the cost of 'bullying' to our society. Although we may be able to estimate the cost of bullying in terms of dollars and cents, how can we estimate the cost of the psychological damage it causes? Carry out a class discussion on this topic.

Activity 38: Genetically modified foods ... who can you believe?

In dealing with controversial issues, often we have to rely on what the 'experts' tell us. Unfortunately, our 'experts' are human beings like everyone else therefore they have their own bias. Where does that leave you and me? How do we make decisions that are informed and balanced? The debate relating to genetically modified (GM) foods between Norman Borlaug and Peter Garrett titled Who can you believe? will clearly show the difficulties that voters and consumers encounter.

You will need the following tools:
- *X chart* (page 114)
- *Venn diagram* (page 112)
- *LDC* (page 100)

Learning activities

- Carry out an *X chart* on Mr Peter Garrett and on Professor Norman Borlaug.

- Compare and contrast the views held by Professor Borlaug and Mr Garrett by using a *Venn diagram*.

- Use the *SOWC* analysis to forecast the long term effect of GM crops.

- Can you explain why Mr Garrett did not mention any potential benefits from using GM crops?

- Can you explain why Professor Borlaug did not mention any possible dangers in using GM crops?

- Is it possible that Professor Borlaug and Mr Garrett are presenting two somewhat 'biased' views of GM foods? Is there room for compromise? Complete an *LDC* on the views held by these two individuals and then generate a third option by integrating the best ideas.

- Do people throughout the world have enough objective data to be able to make informed decisions about GM foods? Prepare your own objective feature article on GM foods and then carry out a debate on this topic with the rest of your class.

- Your job is to advise the world leaders on how to prevent famine. Evaluate the research presently available and then advise them on future developments in GM technology.

- Suppose that in future there will be an outcry against GM foods. Will this favour those countries that can show that their crops are not genetically engineered?

- If GM technology is as good as Professor Borlaug says it is, do we then have the right to deny small scale Third World farmers access to improved seeds, fertilisers and chemicals?

- If GM technology is as bad as Mr Garrett says it is, why is it that some scientists believe that it has such wonderful potential for mankind?

- If you were to interview Professor Borlaug and Mr Garrett today, do you think their views would have changed since the original interview in 1999?

- Can you predict the world's population and the methods used to feed us in the year 2025?

- Suppose that GM crops were to form the basis of our global food supply. Will this mean that eventually the food supply will be controlled by a small number of multinational companies? Is it fair for farmers to have to buy their seeds and pesticides from the same company? Predict possible conflicts of interest.

- Have multinational companies taken out patents on their GM crops? If so, has this led to the extinction of many older varieties of seeds? How dangerous is this to the 'gene pool'?

- Imagine that it is the year 2025. As predicted by Professor Borlaug, the world population has reached 8.3 billion people. In addition, following Mr Garrett's successful campaign, the entire world banned GM technology in 1999. Predict what is likely to happen!

Who can you believe?

Norman Borlaug, was awarded the Nobel Peace Prize in 1970 for his work in developing high-yield wheat, rice and maize whilst working in Mexico under the sponsorship of the Rockefeller Foundation. He is credited to have created the Green Revolution. Professor Borlaug argues that Genetically Modified foods are the only hope for the world's starving population.

According to the article that appeared in The Weekend Australian (December,

1999) he says:

- World population is projected to reach 8.3 billion by 2025 before stabilising at 10 billion towards the end of the next century.

- We can feed 8.3 billion people, if farmers are allowed to use GM technology.

- In order to meet the rapidly growing food needs of the population, we must find new and appropriate technologies to raise cereal crop yields.

- We cannot turn back the clock and only use methods developed to feed a smaller population. It took 10,000 years to expand food production to the present level of 5 billion tonnes per year. By 2025 we will need to nearly double that amount and that cannot be done unless farmers have access to high-yield crop production methods such as GM technology.

- Genetic modification of crops is not some kind of witchcraft. Instead, it enables us to feed the human race by harnessing the forces of nature.

- Today, extremists in the environmental movement from rich nations are doing everything possible to stop scientific progress.

Peter Garrett is the past president of the Australian Conservation Foundation, Midnight Oil lead-singer and presently the Member for Kingsford Smith. Mr Garrett believes that GM foods are extremely dangerous and that we do not need them as we already have enough food to feed the entire planet.

According to the article that appeared in The Weekend Australian (December, 1999) he says:

- The biggest alleged benefit of GM crops is the promise to end world hunger. But world hunger could end today without a single gene being spliced.

- There is enough food to feed the whole planet – now. The world produces nearly 2 kg of food per person per day.

- Just because a country produces enough food to feed its people it doesn't mean that it will happen. Large-scale commercial farming in developing countries is about exporting food to rich countries not feeding the people who grow it.

- Producing more food will not bring an end to hunger. Most likely it will result in producing exciting new dog foods in Los Angeles.

• GM crops do not reduce the use of herbicides. In fact, an OECD investigation revealed that 40% of GM crops were developed to be herbicide-resistant. This means that they will need more, not less herbicides. The associated health effects of herbicides include cancer and harm to our immune system.

Where are we with this discussion in 2006?

Undeniably, the use of Green Revolution-type hybrid strains of wheat, rice, maize and other cereals have produced higher crop yields in India, Pakistan, Philippines, Sri Lanka and other underdeveloped countries.

However, the critics point out that at present we have more than 1 billion people starving in the world. For example, one third of India's 1.1 billion people are poverty-stricken. Since the poor don't have the money to buy food, increased production will not help them in any way. Thus, the government is forced to store millions of tons of foods. Apparently, what we need are social reforms that will address the powerlessness of the poor rather the production of more food.

In addition, the Green Revolution is now coming under attack from environmentalists who argue that the Green Revolution-style farming is not ecologically sustainable thus they are promoting integrated farming or organic farming techniques.

The facts

The Green Revolution relies on:

1. High yielding varieties or hybrid strains of wheat, rice, maize and other cereals.

2. Extensive use of chemical fertilisers.

3. Improved irrigation methods.

4. Use of heavy machinery.

5. Development of pesticides and herbicides.

Thus, what are the achievements of the Green Revolution to date and what are its criticisms?

Supporters of the Green Revolution argue that it has:

1. Saved almost 1 billion lives.

2. Resulted in a three fold increase in rice and wheat production in Asia between 1961–2000. For example, in 1978–79 India for the first time became an exporter of food grains.

3. Led to dramatic increase in crop productivity on existing land, thus saving 2.7 billion acres of land from coming under cultivation.

4. Preserved huge number of wildlife species from extinction.

5. Led to an increase in wildlife on farms due to farming techniques such as tillage that have increased with the introduction of modified crops.

6. Reduced land erosion due to no-till farming.

7. Created a most successful chemical and biotechnology industry led by Monsanto, DuPont and Novartis.

8. Reduced dependency on low-skilled human labour.

Critics argue that by focusing on hybrids and genetically modified crops the Green Revolution has led to:

1. Loss of biodiversity – meaning that by cultivating only a fewer variety of crops we have become exposed to new crop pests which could lead to famine.

2. Health effects – the pesticides and herbicides used in cultivating these crops are toxic to both insects and humans. This is particularly dangerous in Third World countries where the workers are too poor to be able to buy protective clothes.

3. Corporate dependence – many hybrid seeds are sterile, or they are sold to farmers on the condition that they do not save the seeds.

4. Social change – the Green Revolution encouraged large-scale farming which means that small farmers and unskilled labourers no longer can compete. This has led to thousands of people leaving the land and moving into towns and cities thus creating huge slums.

50 Cooperative Learning Activities

5. Fossil fuel dependency – some chemical fertilisers, pesticides and herbicides are derived from fossil fuel thus making agriculture reliant on petroleum products.

6. Fertiliser dependent – high yielding crops require large amounts of fertilisers.

7. Pollution – fertilisers, pesticides and herbicides are polluting rivers and lakes.

8. Land degradation – the Green Revolution destroys soil quality due to increased salinity from heavy irrigation.

Reference: The Weekend Australian, *Between the Tynes,* December 18-19, 1999.

Activity 39: Introducing magnetism to young children

For this activity you will need the following materials:
- bar magnets
- iron filings
- 2 hula hoops
- large table (place it in the middle of the room)
- box full of small items (eg. paper clips, nuts, bolts, plastic pegs, scissors with plastic handles and metal blades, and plastic name tags)
- *Venn diagram* (page 112)
- *LDC* (page 100)

Learning activities

- Hold a bar magnet in your hand, then move it close to the bar magnet that is being held by another student until the two magnets either 'touch' (attract) or push each other away (repel). This is best done on the floor.

- Class discussion – 'What is happening and why?'

- Working in groups of two, place the two bar magnets on the floor near each other. Then, a piece of paper is placed on top of the magnets. Now sprinkle a small amount of iron filings on top of the paper.

- What happens when you move the paper from side to side?

- How far can you lift the paper before the iron filings no longer move? What control this?

- Class discussion – 'How can you explain what you have just seen?'

- The teacher has placed paper clips, nuts, bolts, plastic pegs, scissors with plastic handles and metal blades, and plastic name tags on top of the table. In addition, the teacher has placed on the floor two hula hoops overlapping one another so that they form a *Venn diagram*. Whilst holding a bar magnet, each child walks to the table that has been placed in the middle of the room. As the child walks around the table, they decide which item to 'touch' with the magnet. If the bar magnet 'touches' the item, then it is placed on the left side of the *Venn diagram*. If the bar magnet does not 'touch', the item is placed on the right side of the *Venn diagram*. This continues until there are no items left on the table.

- Class discussion — 'What are you going to put in the middle of the two hula hoops? Why?'

- When you go home this afternoon, look around your house, your parents' car and your bike. Your job is to locate all the places that have small magnets. Make a list to be shared with the class tomorrow.

- Reflect on this activity using an *LDC* thinking tool.

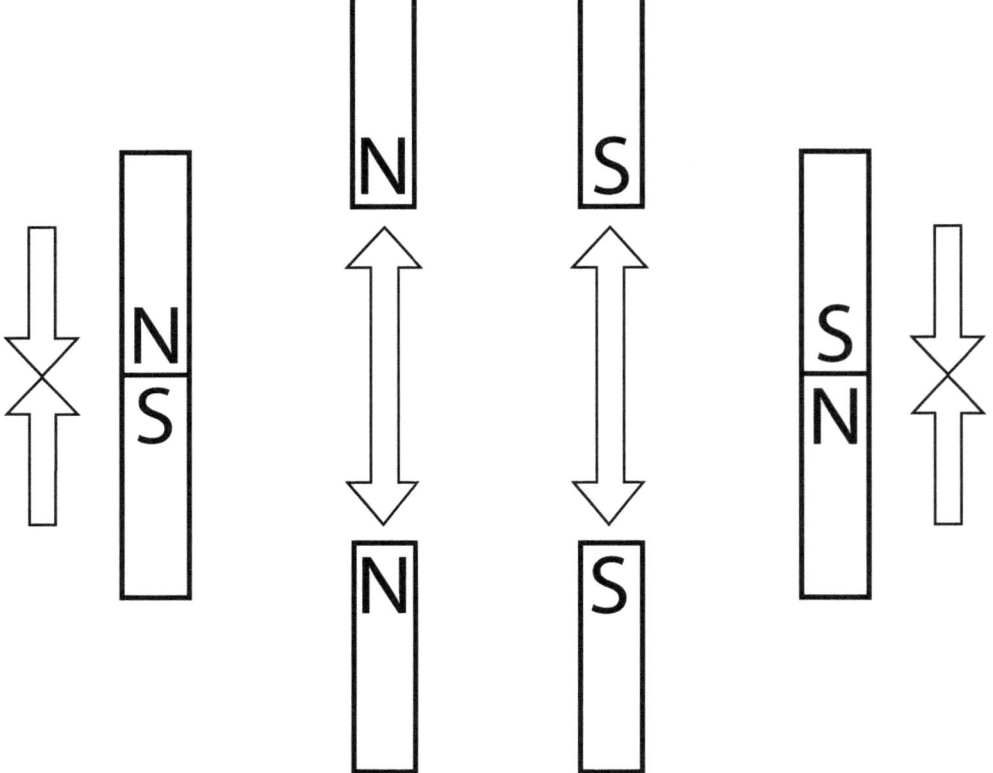

Activity 40: Should scientists be allowed to create a new 'organism'?

Presently, scientists are discovering large number of individual genes that, one day, might enable them to create for the first time a new 'organism' in their laboratory. The President of the World is relying on your advice in order to decide whether or not scientists should be allowed to go ahead with this research.

You will need the following tools:
- *TAP* technique (page 108)
- *SOWC* analysis (page 106)

Learning activities

- You are given a month in which to gather all the relevant data on which to base your advice. What will you do? Who will you turn to? Use *TAP* to brainstorm all the possibilities.

- You have decided to assemble a panel of experts to assist you. Who would you choose to become a member of this panel? On what basis will you be selecting these experts?

- Once you have assembled this panel, carry out a *SOWC* analysis titled 'Should scientists be allowed to develop a new organism?'

- Analyse the data from the *SOWC* analysis and prioritise the issues that are of most concern to you and to the panel.

- Do you have enough reliable data on which to base your advice or do you require additional information? Where will this information come from?

- Based on the data that you have gathered and evaluated to date, what will you advise the President of the World to do?

- Present your report to your class. What thinking tool will you use to receive their feedback?

Activity 41: Why would you want to go to the North Pole?

Read the article titled Caroline Hamilton and the ice girls about the first all-female expedition to the North Pole.

You will need the following tools:
- *X, Y or W charts* (pages 114–116)
- *BROW* (page 98)
- *TREC* (page 107)
- *The Rake* (page 109)

Learning activities

- Why did these four women want to climb the North Pole? Carry out an *X, Y or W chart* or *The Rake* on these women as they stand on the North Pole.

- Imagine what must be like to stand on the North Pole! Use *BROW* to write a letter to your friends/parents/teachers and share with them what you are experiencing whilst you are standing there.

- Prepare a marketing campaign to raise the funds needed for this expedition. Share your campaign with your class.

- You have decided to conquer the South Pole. What would you need to make this expedition successful? Who would you invite to come with you? Why have you chosen these people?

- Working with your group, prepare a daily menu for this expedition. Use *TREC* to calculate what this expedition will cost in food alone?

- Due to bad weather you have to wait six days before you can be picked up at the South Pole. How do you feel? What will you do to keep yourself from freezing?

- You have just completed this unbelievable journey. Share your experiences with your class. How will you do this?

Caroline Hamilton and the ice girls

Caroline Hamilton was a member of the first all-women expedition to the North Pole in the spring of 1997. People who ask "Why do they want to do it" will probably never understand what motivates others to do unbelievable feats.

The idea of going to the North Pole was born in 1995 when Caroline Hamilton asked Pen Hadow, Managing Director of The Polar Travel Co. if an expedition could be organised to enable her to walk to the North Pole. The girls who participated in this expedition were chosen on merit rather than wealth as the funds to carry out this venture were provided by a number of companies headed by McVitie's Penguin biscuits.

The team made up by Caroline Hamilton, Pom Olver, Zoe Hudson and Lucy Roberts and guides Matty McNair and Denise Martin set out from Ward Hunt Island, the northernmost tip of Canada for the North Pole on March, 14, 1997.

> 'Undeniably, this was a gruelling journey as the girls had to survive in an extremely harsh environment with temperatures dropping to -45C. Finally, the team reached the North Pole on May 25, 1997. It is very difficult to describe my feelings on reaching the Pole. It was a mixture of elation and relief. The Ice Girls had done it. Suffice to say it is unlike any other destination where there is something tangible to signify your arrival, whether it be a signpost or a landmark. But at the North Pole there is nothing. The only reason you know you are there is because the GPS tells you, it's very strange. So after planting the flag, reciting the names of all the previous team members and singing "God Save the Queen" (what else?), we set up tent and waited and waited and waited ...'
> (Zoe Hudson).

Activity 42: How is the Internet impacting on you?

The Internet is now part of daily life for most Australians, something that has come about in the past ten years. Sometimes it is important to stop and consider what this means to us personally and reflect upon its impact on our behaviour.

You will need the following tool:
- *SOWC* analysis (page 106)

Learning activities

- The Internet is enabling you to have access to all kinds of information from around the world 24 hours a day. How do you think this is effecting you in terms of:

- The things that you value most in your life?

- The way you behave, dress and think?

- Your relationships with your parents, friends and teachers?

- The freedom to choose what you read and watch?

- The responsibility to choose the material that you access?

- The clothes that you wear and the music that you listen to?

- Your political affiliation and the way that you will vote?

- The sports and the hobbies that you will become involved in?

- The way you stay in touch with your friends and your family?

- Now, imagine what your life would be like if you did not have access to the Internet. Millions of children around the world do not have access to the Internet, particularly those in Third World countries. Does it mean that they are further disadvantaged by this? What can we do to assist these children so that they would be able to access the Internet and hopefully have a brighter future? Carry out a class discussion on this topic.

• Should governments censor individuals and prevent them from placing offensive material on the Internet? For example, how do we stop people from 'trading' pornography, conducting terrorist activity or encouraging discrimination on the basis of gender, colour or religion over the Internet?

• Carry out a *SOWC* analysis titled 'What impact the Internet will have on people by 2020'?

Activity 43: Should fathers take paternity leave?

Ms Cherie Blair, wife of Britain's Prime Minister Tony Blair strongly believed that her husband should take paternity leave upon the birth of their child in 2000. Mrs Blair explained why her husband should follow the example of the Finnish Prime Minister who became the first Finnish government minister to take paternity leave when his wife, Paivi, gave birth to their first child Emilia.

Other European nations have implemented innovative policies that enable people to integrate work and family life. Australian States and Territories are currently enacting laws to enable fathers to take paternity leave. For example, in NSW as of December 19, 2005 extra parental leave arrangements will apply for working parents on awards including paternity leave of up to one week taken at the time of birth and a further period of unbroken leave taken in order to be the child, primary care giver.

You will need the following tools:
- *SOWC* analysis (page 106)
- *TAP* technique (page 108)
- *Venn diagram* (page 112)

Learning activities

- Gather some resources to help you complete the following questions and activities:

- Do you think that fathers should take paternity leave?

- How do you feel about this issue? Form a small group and share your thoughts with them.

- With the group, carry out a SOWC analysis titled 'Should fathers take paternity leave?'.

- Research then compare and contrast a father that has taken paternity leave with a father that has not, using the *Venn diagram*.

- Suppose you were an employer, how would you feel about having to provide paternity leave? Split the class in half and use *TAP* to carry out a class debate on this issue.

- Did Prime Minister Tony Blair take paternity leave upon the birth of his child? Do you think he made the right decision? Why?

- Even though governments are passing laws that allow fathers to take paternity leave, explain why so few men take advantage of these opportunities.

Activity 44: The 'magical' potato

For this activity teachers will need to prepare the following:
- 2 buckets
- water
- potatoes
- salt
- groups of four students
- *PSDR* method (page 104)
- *WINCE* strategy (page 113)
- *TAP* technique (page 108)

Learning activities

- When you enter the classroom you will observe two identical buckets on the teacher's desk, both with the same amount of water in them.

    Bucket A: A potato is resting on the bottom of the bucket.

    Bucket B: A potato is floating in the water near the top of the bucket.

- Is there something 'strange' about what you have observed?

- Based on what you have already learned by doing Activity 23, how can you explain this? The *PSDR* method may be of some assistance to you!

- Your challenge now is to generate your own 'model' so that you can explain why the potato sinks in Bucket A and floats near the top in Bucket B.

- Use the *WINCE* thinking tool to devise an experiment that will allow you to float the potato half way between the bottom and the top of the bucket. The materials that you can use are: buckets, water, potatoes and salt. No strings or weights can be used to hold the potato in the middle of the bucket and the level of the water must be 2 cm below the lid. Hint: Review what you already know about water!

- Did you manage to float the potato in the middle of the bucket whilst the level of the water is 2 cm below the lid? Present your experiment to your class.

- Was the *WINCE* strategy of any assistance to you? In relation to this experiment, is there a better thinking tool that you could have used instead of the *WINCE* strategy?

- Brainstorm using *TAP* all the other methods that you could have used to float the potato in the middle of the bucket whilst the level of the water is 2 cm below the lid.

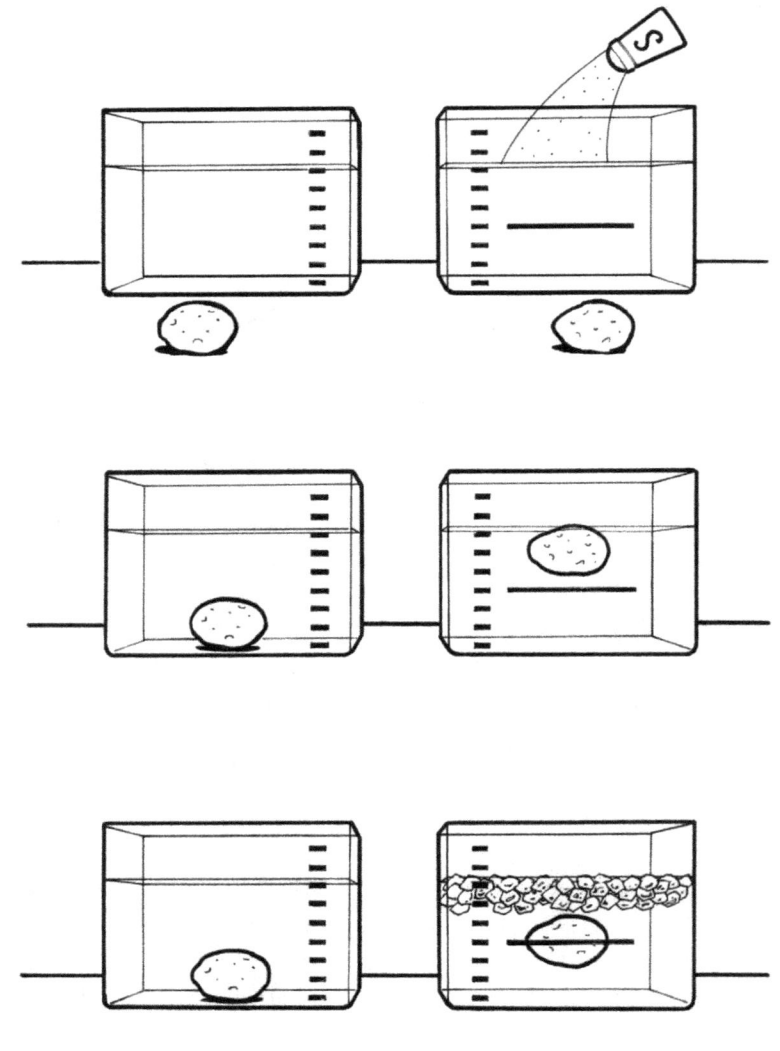

Activity 45: Design, build and test your own rocket

For this activity, you will need the following materials:
- an old film canister
- vinegar
- bicarbonate of soda
- small plastic cup (50 ml)
- teaspoon
- plastic bottle with some water
- *SOWC* analysis (page 106)

Learning activities

- Consider the materials you have to use, plan and build your rocket then complete the following questions and activities:
    - How much vinegar and bicarbonate of soda will you need to build your own rocket? Will this ratio remain constant regardless of the experiment?
    - How far did your rocket travel?
    - How long did your rocket take to travel this distance?
    - Are you able to calculate its speed?
    - What caused the top of the film canister to 'fly'?
    - How useful was this activity in understanding basic laws of chemistry?
    - How could this experiment be related back to Newton's Law?
- Once you have completed these activities, then you should prepare a Marketing Plan for your rocket.
- You may decide to use the *SOWC* analysis as a starting point for your Marketing Plan.
- In order to celebrate the completion of this Project, present your Marketing Plan to your class.

Activity 46: Testing foods (for young children)

For this activity you will need a small plate, a small bottle of iodine and a thin slice of the following foods:

- potato
- lettuce
- banana
- white bread
- carrot
- pear
- apple

As well as the following tools:
- *W chart* (page 114)
- *The Rake* (page 109)
- *PSDR* method (page 104)
- *Thinking clouds* (page 103)

Learning activities

- How do you feel when you have a very tasty meal? Complete either the *W chart* or *The Rake*.

- Students share their work with their group then discuss the question 'Why do we eat?' making their ideas into a *Thinking cloud*.

- Fold an A4 piece of paper into three equal parts.

- Label these three parts as follows: (left) List A, (centre) Testing Foods and (right) List B.

- Use the *PSDR* method to predict which of the foods have the most amount of starch.

- Under List A, draw up seven lines and place the number 1 to 7. Then, list the foods from the one that you think has the most starch to the one that that you think has the least amount of starch. Place the name of these foods next to the appropriate number.

- So, how do we know how much starch is found in different foods? One way to get a rough idea is to test them with a chemical called Iodine. This chemical is normally yellow-purple in colour but changes to black when it comes in contact with starch. Note: Iodine will stain your clothes.

- Now, you are ready to do some testing. Place one slice of each food on the plate and then add one drop of iodine to each food. Watch what happens! Do you see any change in colour? What does this mean?

- Draw the plate and the foods in the centre of your page (this is optional).

- Under List B, draw up seven lines and place the number 1 to 7. Then, look at the plate and list the foods from the one that has changed colour the most to the one that has changed colour the least. Place the name of these foods next to the appropriate number.

- Is there a difference between List A and List B? Explain.

Follow-up activities

- Visit your local shopping centre. Read the information that is found on packaged foods such as cereals. Of what value is this information to us? If you had high blood pressure or diabetes how critical would this information be to you?

- Keep a diary of all the types and the amounts of foods that you eat during the next week. Graph this data and share your graph with your group. Are all the children's graphs the same? Carry out a class discussion.

- Based on your knowledge, now prepare the most nutritious and affordable menu for your family for one day or a week.

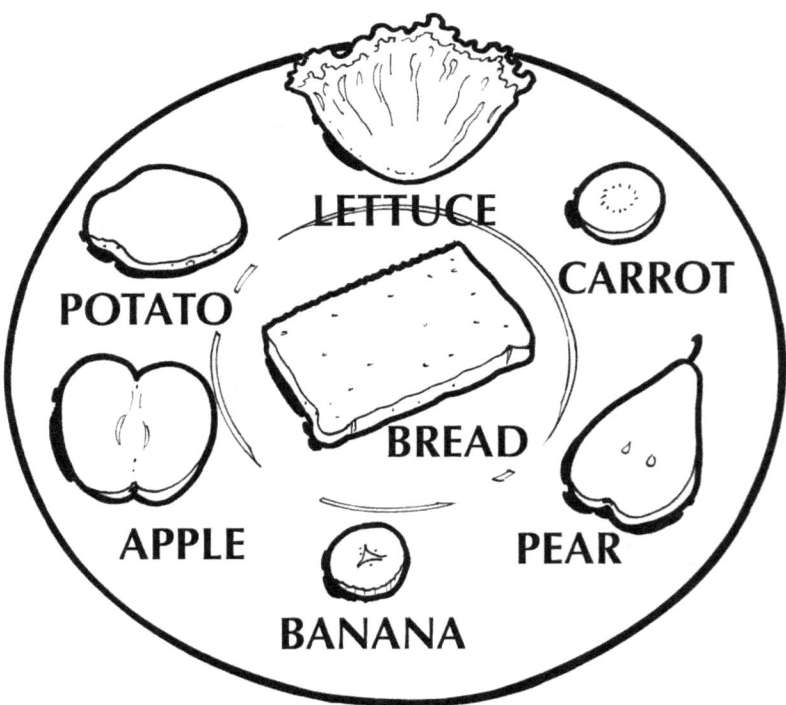

Activity 47: Design, build and test your own bridge

For this activity, you will need the following:
- 100–150 plastic straws
- glue gun loaded with glue
- 2 pieces of timber (20 cm x 20 cm)
- masking tape
- a book weighing 500 g
- photographs of various types of bridges
- *TAP* technique (page 108)
- *SCRAM* (page 105)

Learning activities

- Each team is to build the most inexpensive bridge (1.5 m tall and 1m wide) that will hold a book weighing 500 g. The cost of the materials and labour will be charged as follows:

    - plastic straw = 5 cents each
    - roll of tape = $2.50 each
    - block of wood = $1.50 each
    - hiring of glue gun = $1.00 per hour
    - labour = $5.00 per hour/per person

- Commence this activity by working in groups of four students. Brainstorm using *TAP* which type of bridge you would like to build.

- Each student draws the plans for their bridge. Then, the group decides which of the four bridges will be built.

- Now, divide the original group into two equal groups. Group A and Group B will commence their half bridge from two opposite starting points. The idea is for the two teams to meet halfway in order to link the bridge and to celebrate the completion of their project.

- Each group begins by placing a piece of wood (20 cm x 20 cm) on top of a table. This table should be about 1m wide. Mark a cross at each corner of the wood making certain that the distance between the crosses is about 16 cm.

- Then, add a small amount of glue on each of the four crosses. Before the glue has the opportunity to dry, stand a plastic straw in it. Hold the plastic straw upright until the glue has set. This takes a few seconds. Repeat this until each corner has a plastic straw standing in it.

• Strengthen your foundation by running plastic straws across the four 'pillars' and use a small amount of tape to hold them together.

• To continue the building process, take a new plastic straw, press slightly at the ends and insert it into one of the existing 'pillars'. Use a small amount of tape to hold the two straws together. Continue doing this until your bridge is 1.5 m tall. Remember to strengthen your bridge as you progress otherwise it will bend and fall apart.

• You are now ready to build the platform and hopefully half way you will meet the other members of your team.

• Congratulations! You are now ready to test the bridge by placing a book weighing 500 g, flat on top of your platform. Is your bridge able to support this book? Try heavier books to find out the heaviest book that your bridge will support.

• Calculate how much your bridge cost to build by using the prices stated above. How does your cost compare with the other teams?

• Investigate the possibility of reducing the costs of building your bridge and improving its strength by using *SCRAM*.

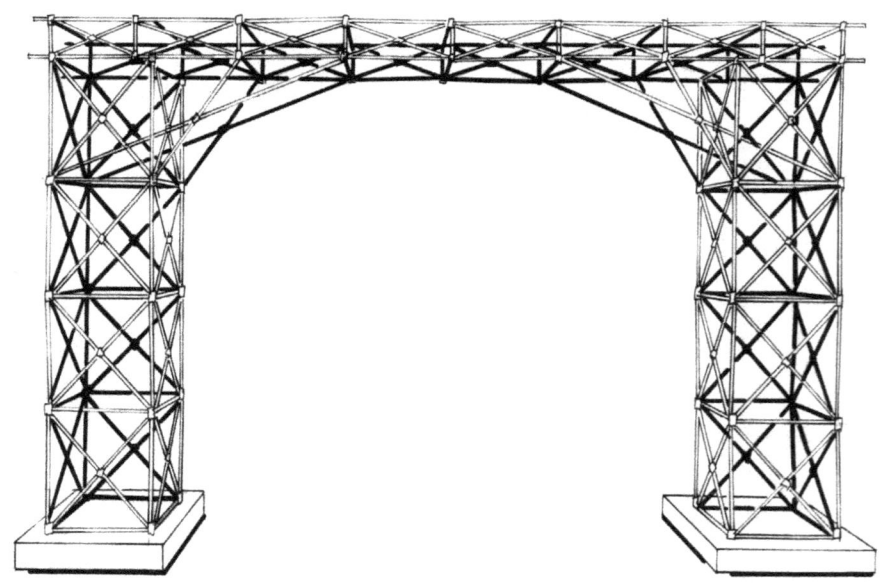

Activity 48: Saving the panda

The giant panda is one of nature's most delightful, beloved and unusual animals. It is also one of the most endangered species in the world.

Your task is to create your own portfolio of work titled 'Saving the Panda' from the following activities. Please note that you will not be expected to complete all the activities. Your teacher will select those that you must complete (core activities) and you can negotiate the others from the 'learning menu' (electives activities).

You will need the following tools:
- *BROW* (page 98)
- *TREC* (page 107)
- *The Rake* (page 109)
- *TAP* technique (page 108)
- *W chart* (page 114)
- *SOWC* analysis (page 106)

Learning activities

- Visit the following websites:

    www.sandiegozoo.org

    www.pandasinternational.org

    www.giantpandabear.com

    www.aza.org/ConScience/PandaJob

    www.wwf.org

- Why has the World Wildlife Fund (WWF) chosen the panda for its logo?

- What is the current estimate of the panda's population?

- Draw a map to show where most panda live today.

- How does the area in which the panda live today differ from the areas that were available to them 50 years ago?

- Why has the area available to the panda decreased so much during the last 50 years?

- State 3 main factors that contribute to the small panda population.

- How would you sell the idea of preserving the panda?

- Arrange a poster to save the panda.

- Using the *BROW* strategy, prepare a newspaper/radio/TV ad to protect the panda.

- If it is going to cost so much money, why should we prevent the panda from becoming extinct? Use *TREC* to calculate how much it will cost to keep the panda from becoming extinct.

- Choose a song about people caring for the environment and explain its meaning to your group.

- Select the music that you will play whilst presenting your Action Plan to your class.

- Pantomime pandas as they grow using *The Rake*.

- Compose a rhythm to save the panda.

- Act and choreograph a dance about saving the panda's habitat.

- Use *TAP* to brainstorm all the things that you can do to prevent the panda from extinction. Now, categorise the things that you can actually do.

- Create and perform a play dealing with clearing bamboo forests.

- Devise an environmental game that could be used to teach others.

- Use *The Rake* to design the best environment for the panda.

- You are standing in front of a panda whilst its habitat is being destroyed. Now, complete a *W chart*.

- Write an autobiography titled 'A day in the life of a panda'.

- Assess whether the panda will be extinct by the year 2020 by using the *SOWC* analysis

Activity 49: What will you do?

It is 3.15 p.m. and you and your best friend are walking home. As a car approaches you, the driver stops the car, winds down the window and asks you politely 'Could you please tell me how to get to this school? I was supposed to be there at 3.00 p.m. but somehow I got lost'. You noticed that the car has a rental sticker on its rear window.

You will need the following tools:
- *X or Y charts* (pages 115–116)
- *TPSS method* (page 110)
- *TAP technique* (page 108)
- *ARC strategy* (page 97)

Learning activities

- Use *X or Y chart* to visualise this person. Share your work with your group using *TPSS* method.

- Now, how are you going to respond to this person's plea for assistance?

- Brainstorm all the choices available to you using *TAP* and then mind map your choices.

- For each available choice, apply the *ARC* strategy.

- Based on the results from the *ARC* strategy, decide on the course of action that you will take and justify your decision.

- What have you learned from doing this activity?

Activity 50: Did the US government do the 'right' thing by returning Elian Gonzales to his father in Cuba?

On November 22, 1999, Elizabeth Brotons, her son Elian, her common-law husband and 11 Cubans tried to flee Cuba on a small boat bound for the US. On November 25, fishermen found the body of a woman near Ft. Lauderdale. Soon after, two men were also found off the coast of the USA holding on a tyre tube and a little later, a child appeared in the ocean clinging to an inner tyre tube. This was Elian Gonzales.

Please read the story of Elian Gonzales.

You will need the following:
- *TAP* technique (page 108)
- *The Rake* (page 109)
- *X, Y or W charts* (pages 114–116)
- *SOWC* analysis (page 106)

Learning activities

- Read the story of Elian Gonzales. Then, in small groups of two or three, complete the following questions:

- Why would Elizabeth Brotons risk her life and her son's life in trying to escape from Cuba? Use *TAP* to brainstorm all possibilities.

- Carry out an *X, Y or W chart* or *The Rake* on Elian whilst he was stranded for hours in the ocean.

- Suppose you were the Attorney General of the US, on what basis did you decide to send Elian back to Cuba? Use *SOWC* analysis to help you in making this decision.

- What long-term impact do you believe this will have on Elian?

- Where is Elian today?

- Do you think this is where he wants to be? Why?

- Do people have the right to live in a country where they will not be persecuted based on ethnic, religious or political reasons? What do you think?

- Carry out a class debate titled 'How should Australia treat its refugees?'

Elian Gonzales

A five-year old Cuban boy, Elian Gonzales is found alone on Thanksgiving Day, November 25, 1999 clinging to an inner tyre tube three miles off the coast of Ft. Lauderdale, Florida. He was one of just three survivors of a group of 14 Cubans who had set off from Cardenas, a coastal town 129 km east of Havana, Cuba on November 22, 1999 in search of freedom and a better life. They were hoping to reach the US in a handmade boat. However, the voyage turned into disaster when 56 km from the US coast, the boat ran into a storm. Elizabeth Brotons, Elian's mother and 11 others drowned.

The fishermen that found Elian took him to hospital for treatment and he was released the next day into the custody of his uncle, Lazaro Gonzalez and other relatives in Miami. Meanwhile, the Cuban government sent a note to the US mission in Havana requesting Elian's return to Cuba and Juan Miguel, Elian's father filed a complaint with the UN to get custody of his son. Then, attorneys for Elian's relatives in Miami filed a request for his political asylum. Rallies and protest marches followed both in Miami and in Cuba thus, Elian found himself in a tug-of-war between Cuba and the US.

On April 19, 2000 the 11th US Circuit Court of Appeals granted a request by Elian's Miami relatives to block his return to Cuba. However, three days later on April 22, 2000 in a pre-dawn raid, armed US federal agents seized Elian from the home of his Miami relatives and he was united with his father a few hours later. Then, on June 1, 2000 a federal appeals court upholds the US government's authority to deny Elian a hearing for political asylum. Finally, Elian Gonzalez and his father arrived in Cuba to a jubilant reception on June 28, 2000.

THINKING TOOLS

- The *TPSS* method was adapted by the author from the original *TPS* method created by Professor Frank Lyman.

- Permission to use the *Jigsaw* thinking tool was given by Professor Elliot Aronson.

- The *Venn diagram*, *SOWC* analysis and *X* and *Y charts* have been adapted by the author.

- For further information on using the thinking tools please refer to *Improving Thinking in the Classroom* (2005), Ralph Pirozzo, Hawker Brownlow Education, Victoria.

- The author acknowledges the ground-breaking work carried out by Tony Buzan and Nancy Margulies in relation to Mind Maps.

ARC strategy

Action	Reaction	Consequences
What will you do now?	How will the other person react?	What will be the outcomes?

BROW

A thinking strategy to encourage children to write

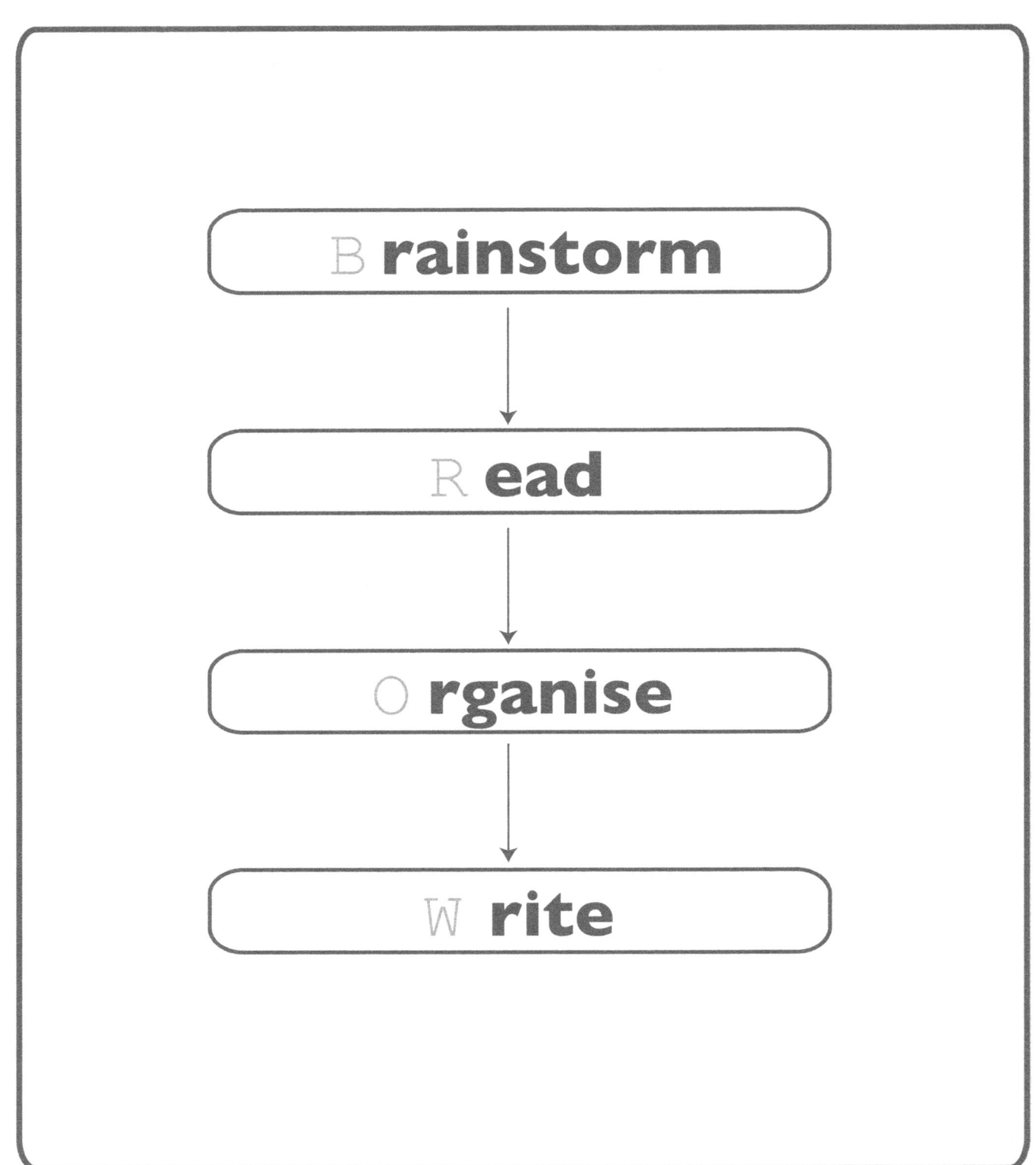

My area of control: dealing with conflict

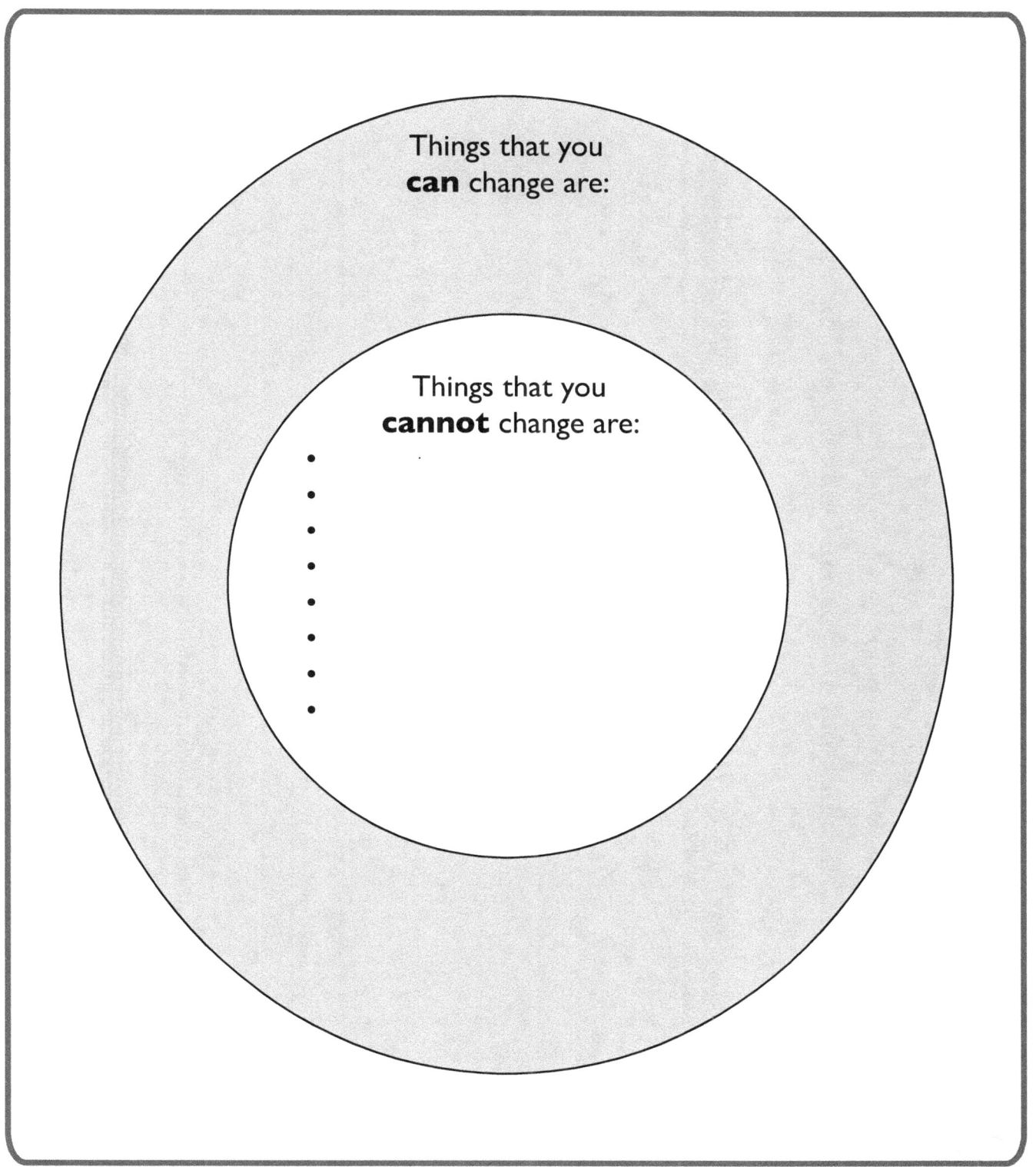

Things that you **can** change are:

Things that you **cannot** change are:
-
-
-
-
-
-
-

50 Cooperative Learning Activities

LDC

Like	Dislike	Challenging

Introducing children to multiple intelligences

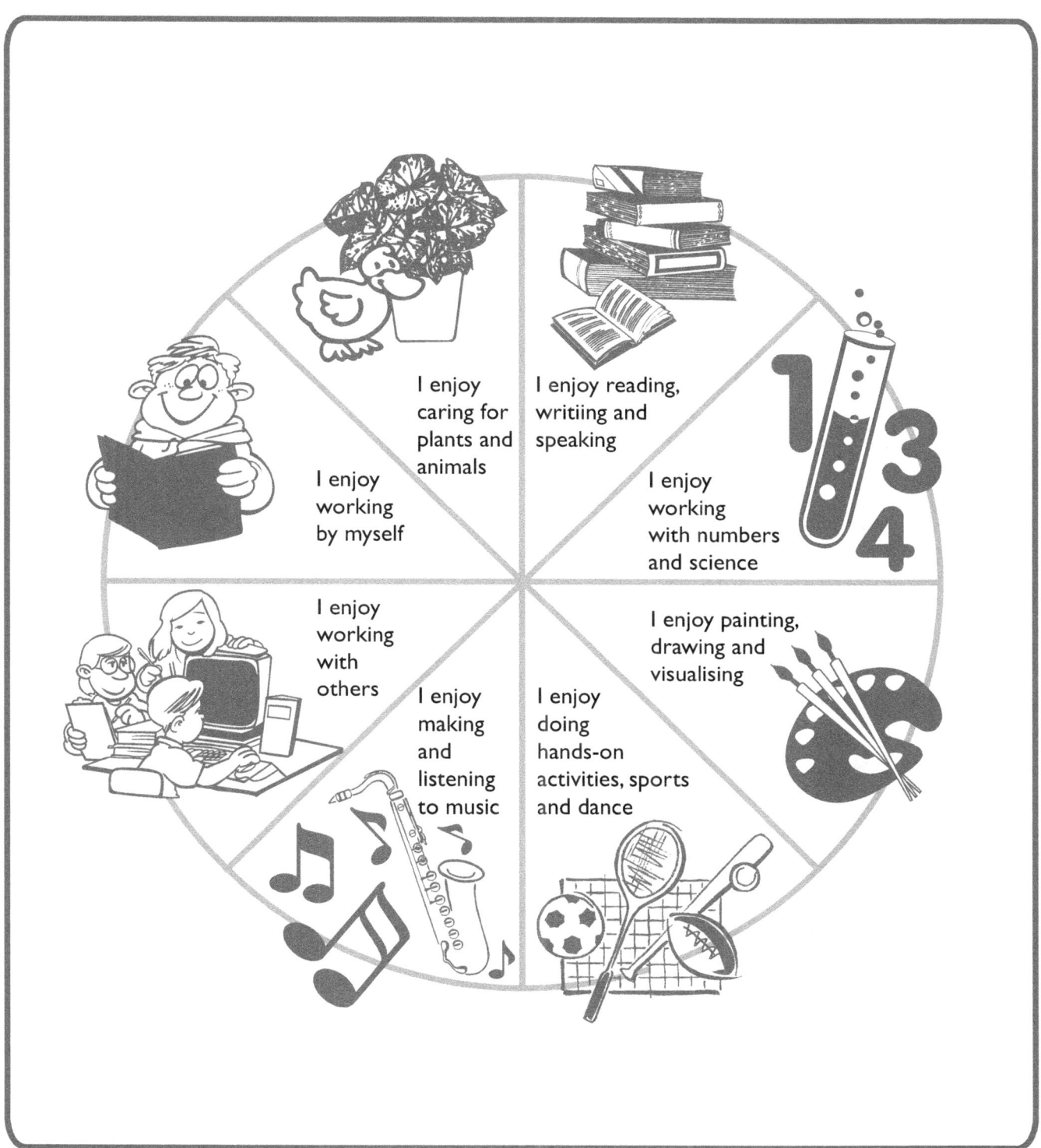

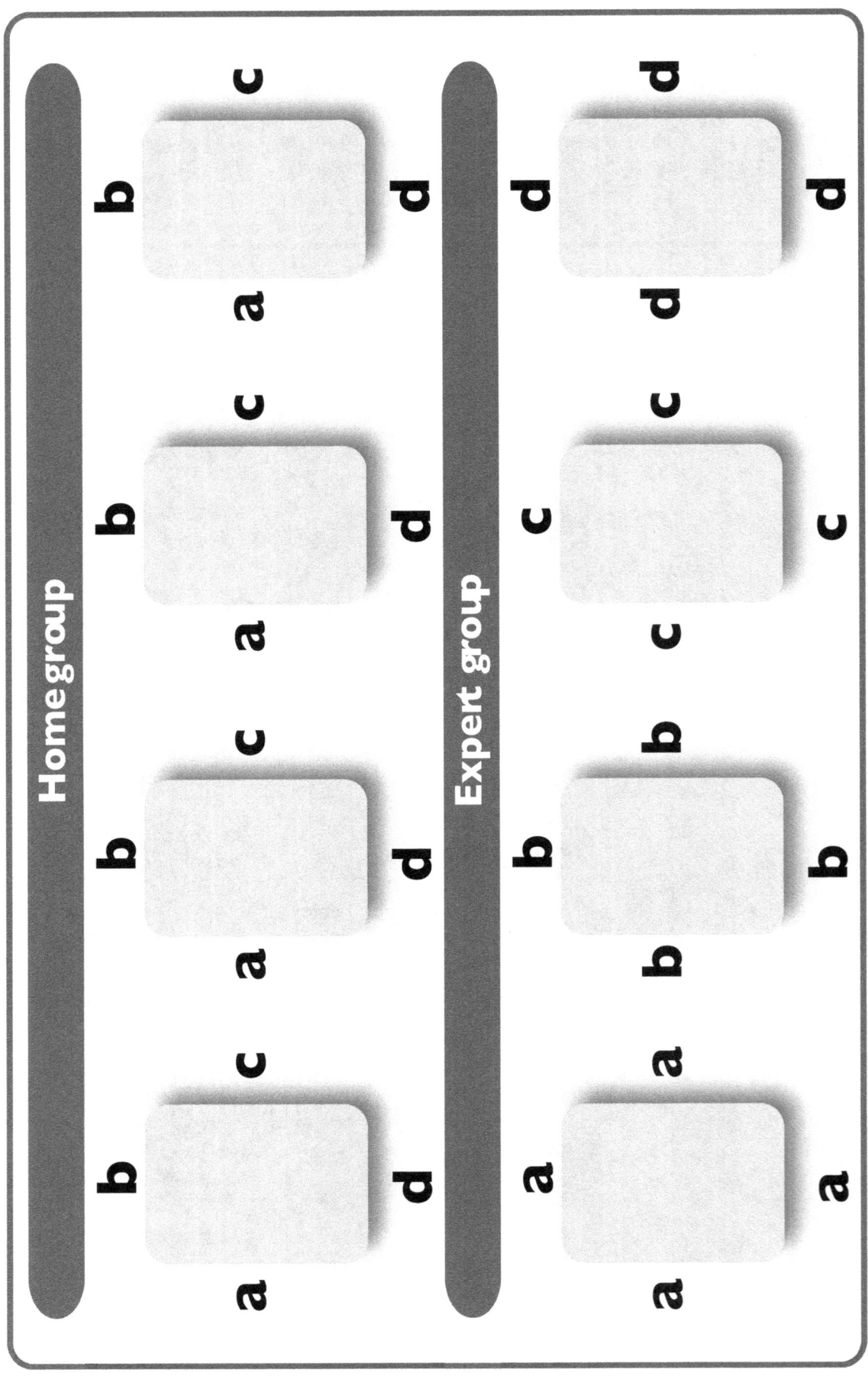

Thinking clouds

50 Cooperative Learning Activities

The PSDR method

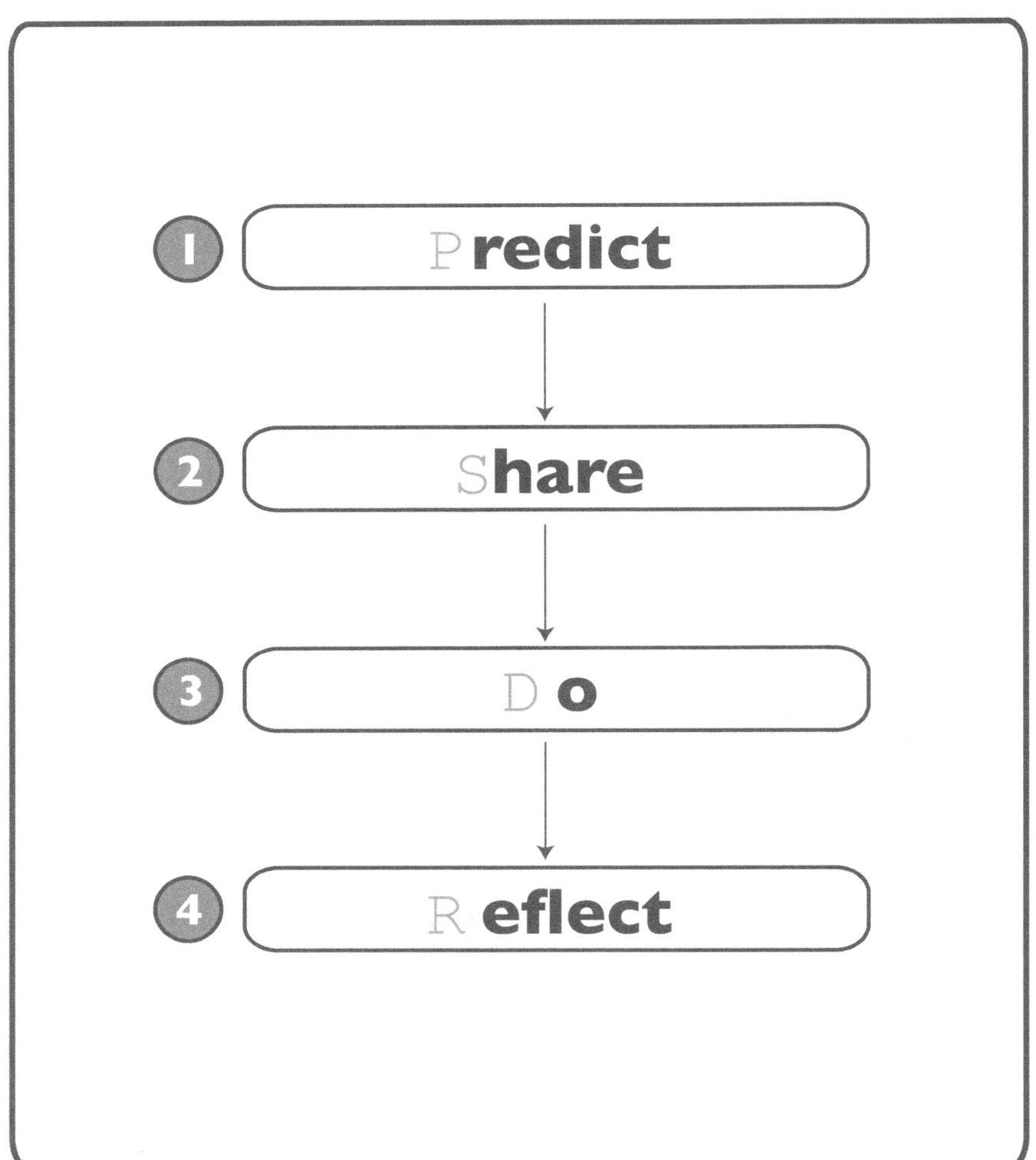

SCRAM

Possible verbs that can be used with this strategy are:

S	**C**	**R**	**A**	**M**
Substitute	Combine	Rate	Adapt	Modify
Separate	Classify	Report	Act	Magnify
Solve	Compare	Research	Advise	Make
Suggest	Complete	Restate	Analyse	Mime
Survey	Compose	Review	Apply	Minimise
	Conduct	Rewrite	Argue	
	Construct		Arrange	
	Contrast		Assess	
	Create		Audition	

SOWC analysis

Strengths	Opportunities	Weaknesses	Consequences

TREC

Think	Read	Estimate	Calculate
Get your brain into action.	Read the question.	Estimate what you believe the answer should be.	Carry out the calculations required.
When working with mathematics, what do we normally do?	If you do not understand it, read it again.	Is your estimate similar to your team members?	How close is your answer to your estimation?
	Ask your teacher for assistance.		How do you know that you have the right answer?

TAP technique

The Rake

Whilst moving around your new place, list the following:

Touch	Smell	Taste	Look	Listen	Feel	Think
What do the objects feel like?	What do they smell like?	What does it taste like?	What do you see?	What sounds can you hear like?	How do you feel?	What are you thinking?

The TPSS method

1. **T**hink
2. **P**air
3. **S**hare
4. **S**quare

The engaging wheel

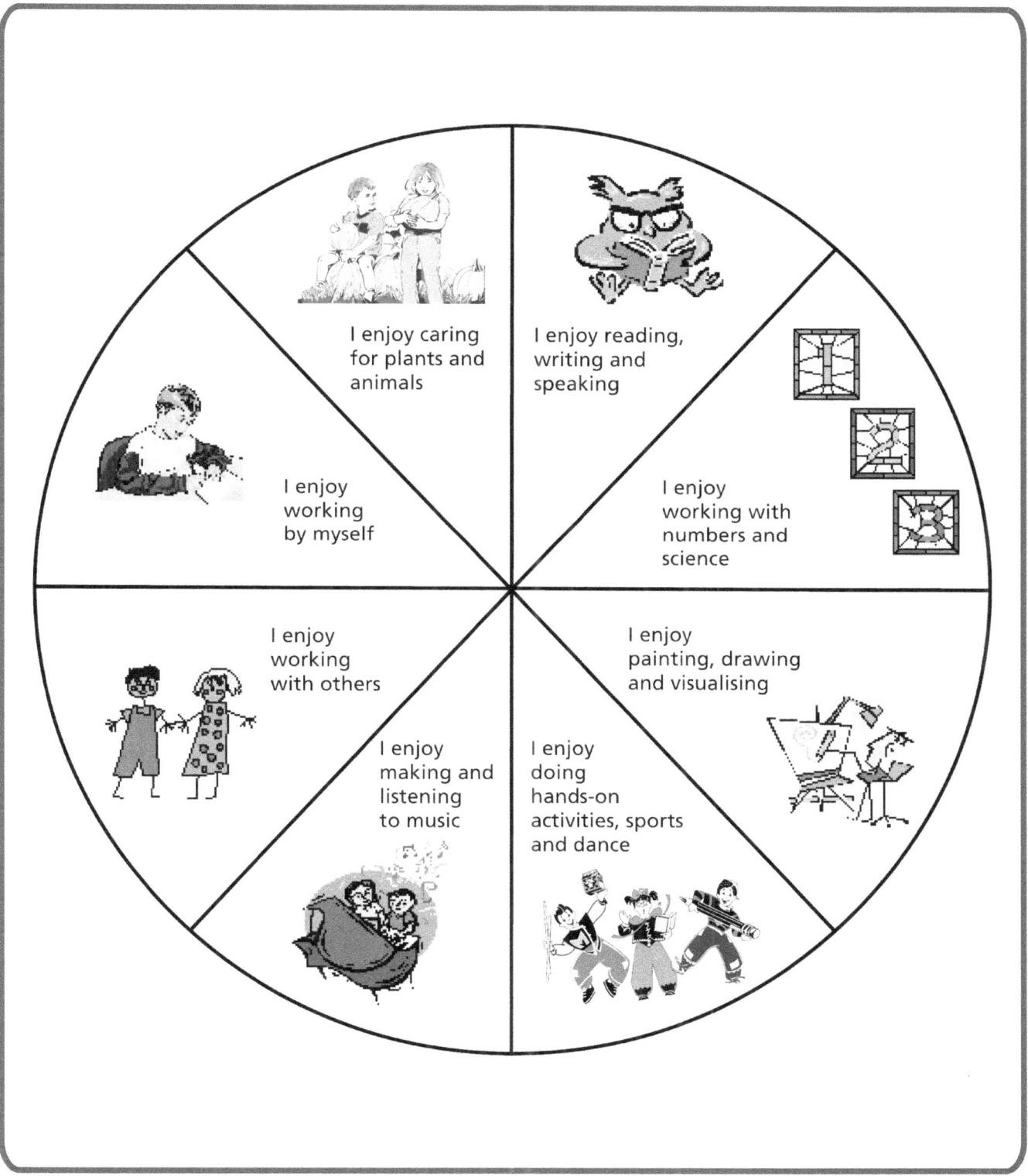

50 Cooperative Learning Activities

Venn diagram

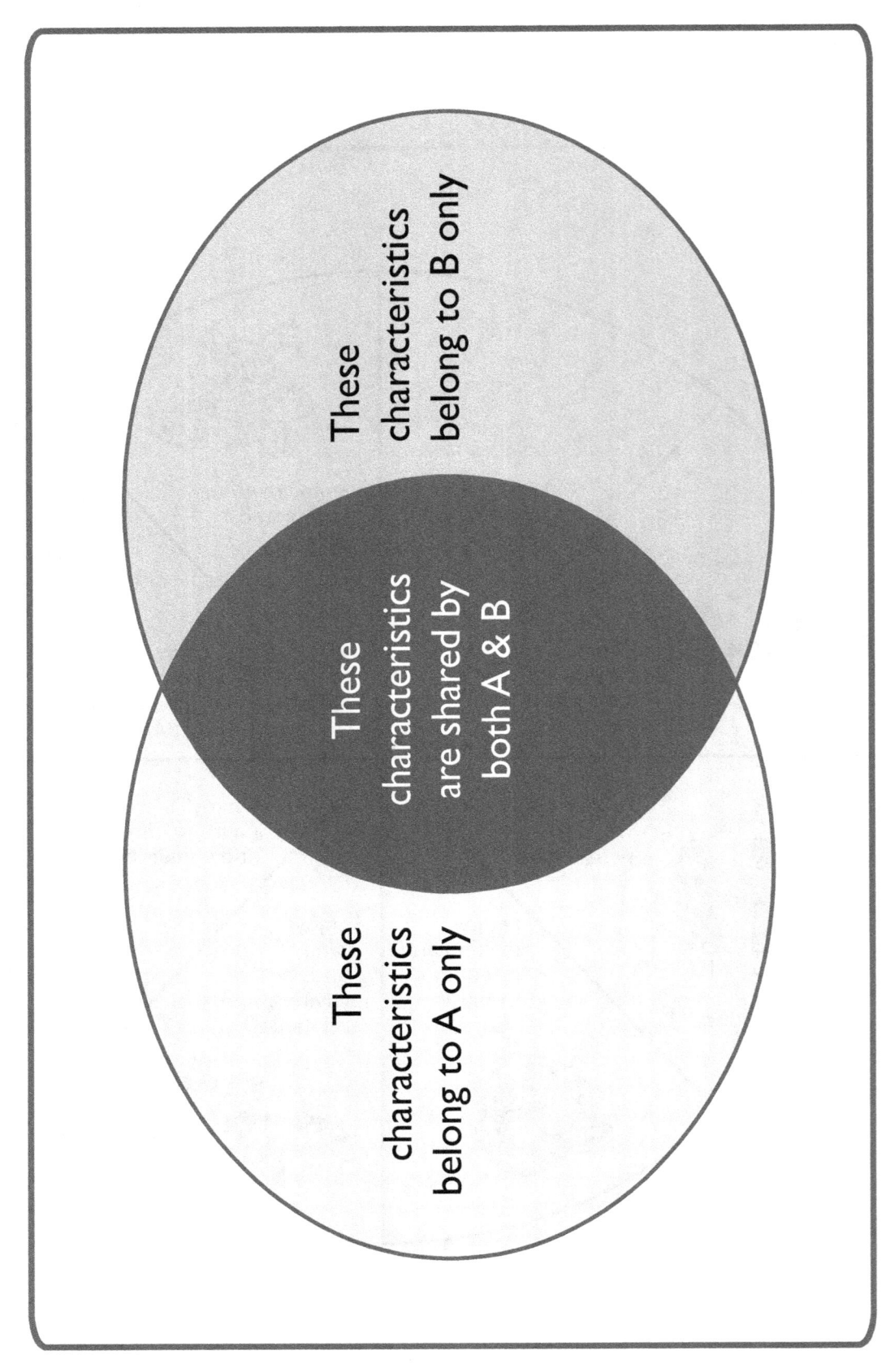

WINCE strategy

Want	Identify	Need	Create	Evaluate
What do I **want** to know?	**Identify** what I already know?	What additional information do I **need**?	What have I **created**?	What have I learned from **evaluating** this activity?

W chart

Looks like	Feels like	Sounds like	Tastes like	Thinks like

X chart

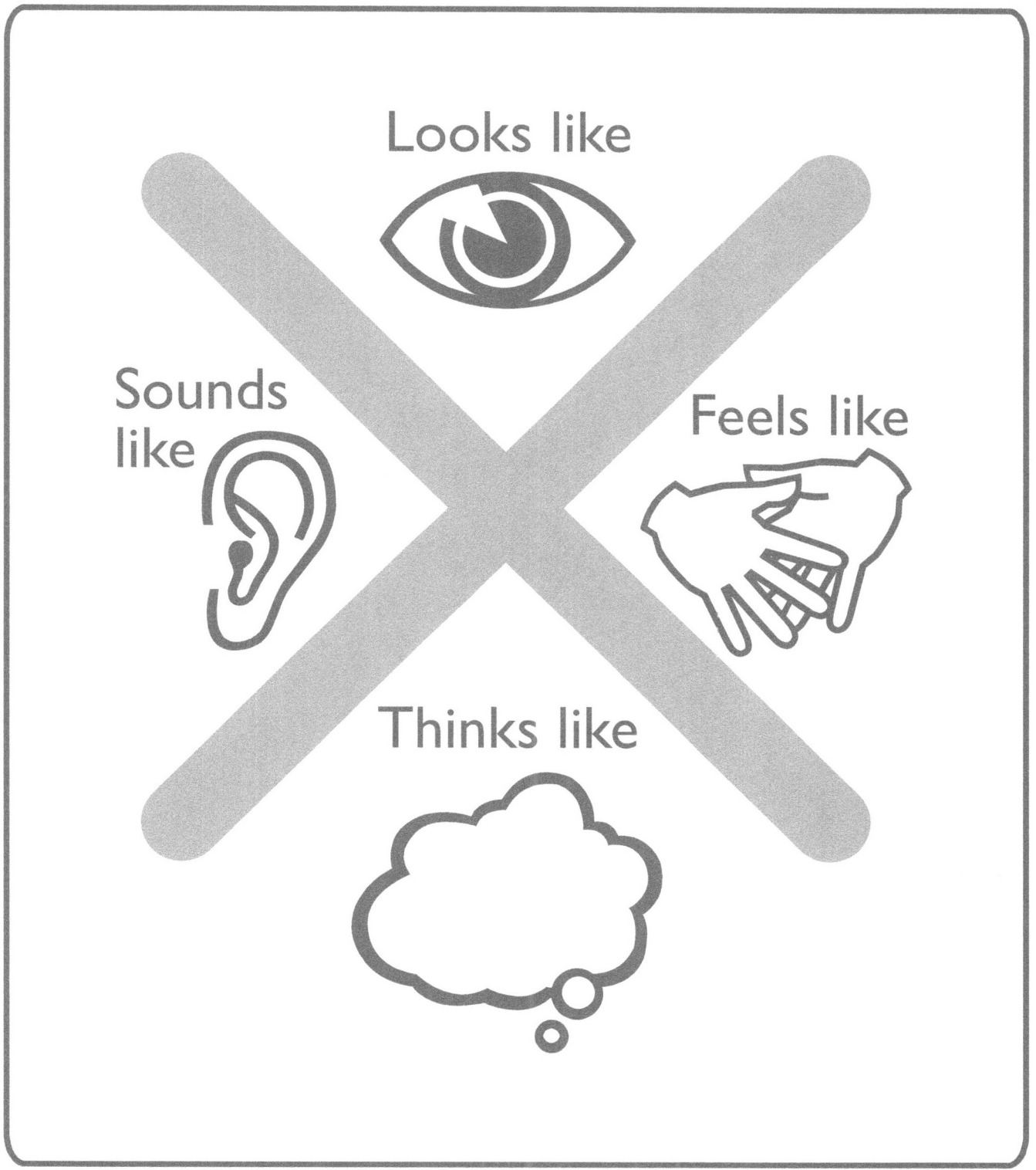

www.ingramcontent.com/pod-product-compliance
Lightning Source LLC
Chambersburg PA
CBHW081918090526
44590CB00019B/3394